THROWING UP RAINBOWS RECOVERY GUIDE

18 Secrets to Freedom From Your Eating Disorder
A Companion to Throwing Up Rainbows

Z ZOCCOLANTE

Copyright © 2019 by Z Zoccolante

All rights reserved. In accordance with the U.S. Copyright Act of 1976, no part of this book may be reproduced in any form or by any electronic or mechanical means, including information storage and retrieval systems, without written permission from the author, except for the use of brief quotations in a book review. If you would like to use material from the book (other than for review purposes) prior written consent must be obtained by contacting the publisher. Thank you for your support of the author's rights.

Dream Big Books
PO BOX 1594
El Segundo, CA 90245
www.dreambigbooks.love
info@dreambigbooks.love

Library of Congress Control Number: 2019915614

ISBN: 978-1-7324536-3-0 (print)
ISBN: 978-1-7324536-5-4 (Kindle)
ISBN: 978-1-7324536-4-7 (epub)

Printed in the United States of America

For all of us, who cracked ourselves open to let the light in.
May we shine.
May your body be home for constellations of stars.

CONTENTS

Introduction vii

1 Honesty & Root Feelings 1
2 Hope 6
3 Choice 10
4 Wants & Don't Wants 16
5 Boundaries & Self-Advocating 20
6 Is This True? 26
7 God 32
8 Sexual Abuse & Eating Disorders 38
9 Becoming Friends With the Feminine 42
10 Models & The Media 46
11 Worth 50
12 What Do You Really Want? 55
13 Trust 61
14 Secrets 65
15 Affirmations 70
16 Relationships 75
17 How to Find a Therapist You Love 84
18 Somatic (Body-Based) Therapies 93
19 The Beauty of the Chaos 102

Acknowledgements 107

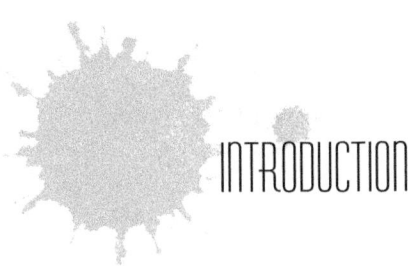

INTRODUCTION

Aloha. I'm Z Zoccolante. For 11 years, I had a secret eating disorder. It crept like a shadow, invading every corner of my life, stealing my joy and whispering sweet you'll-be-nothings.

Now I'm free and happy, and I want to share my secrets of freedom with you.

IF YOU'RE HOLDING THIS BOOK

If you're holding this book, there's a part of you that wants your life back. No matter how small that part is, it believes in the possibility of recovering from your eating disorder. That part believes in the possibility of freedom and happiness.

This guide will help you start important conversations, both with yourself and within your recovery groups. It will also likely spark insights you can choose to share and discuss with those whom you choose to support you in recovery.

As we begin, it's important to understand that people with eating disorders are intelligent. We feel things deeply, often to the point of wanting to numb out. Keep in mind that at one time, the eating disorder was an important solution to deal with the stress or trauma in our life. At first, the disorder might have appeared as a friend, maybe even a lover, but eventually it became an abuser. The temporary solution became the problem.

When this happens, the eating disorder controls our lives and ruins relationships. At this point, we may finally seek help. Yet as we begin the path of recovery, it can feel as though we're inept at untying a huge, knotted ball of yarn.

If we're so smart, then why can't we just figure it out?

RECOVERY IS A PROCESS

When I began my journey, I sought a magic fix to expedite the process. I wanted to find the right key, unlock my cage, and have it be gone. I wanted to be free and happy but recovery loomed over the horizon, out of sight. I wasn't sure I'd ever make it there.

The truth is, recovery is difficult. It's uncomfortable to face, examine, and change your patterns and thoughts. At times it's going to suck, and you're might wonder if it's worth it.

A therapist once told me, "It can't be worse that what you're doing to yourself right now."

I thought, "Good point. OK, what the hell? Why not try?"

The path to recovery is different for everyone, because we each have different life experiences. However, we are connected in this. We share similar sufferings and a longing to be free. When you keep moving forward, even at a snail's pace, freedom and happiness will one day be yours.

We wouldn't put a seed in the ground and then get angry because it didn't grow into a tree overnight. It takes time to grow and relearn how to be without the eating disorder. Be patient with yourself and your growth.

WE ALL HAVE BLACK HOLES

Through my recovery, I realized that there were amazing parts of my life, and there were also holes. These metaphorical holes were lessons and skills I didn't learn growing up.

Eventually I realized the following: it's not about being smart; it's about being equipped. We don't know what we don't know. And we can't know what we've never been taught.

As a teen, I wandered around with these metaphorical gaping holes in my body. This left me prime for some disorder, such as anorexia and bulimia. Disorders love black holes; it's where they build their nests.

Each chapter of this recovery guide walks you through one of these gaping holes. You will have the opportunity to discover, learn, and fill the empty spaces with new skills. Some chapters may resonate more than others. Let them. Everything has a purpose, and whatever works best for you does so for a reason. You don't need to know why.

CREATING YOUR TOOLBOX

At the end of this guide, you'll have a number of new shiny tools to add to your recovery toolbox. When concerns arise along your recovery path, you'll be able to address them with the nifty tools you'll acquire, instead of relying on the solo screwdriver, your eating disorder, that you used to unsuccessfully use to patch every issue. You'll be amazed at how much better you can address issues in your life when you bring working tools to the table.

Again, learning and using new tools/skills takes time. Be patient and kind with yourself as you embody a new way of being. And know that each time you practice, your brain lays down a new neural pathway. Pretty soon you'll have healthy, happy roads to travel down.

May these pages be a gift of insight and forward locomotion on your journey towards recovery.

You can do this. I believe in you.

With Love & Aloha,
Z ;)

P.S – Most likely you've discovered this guide through reading my eating disorder recovery memoir, *Throwing Up Rainbows: My Eating Disorder and Other Colorful Things*, available on Amazon. It's the tell-all, raw and wild truth of the secrets I used to hide. It's not necessary to have read it to delve into this recovery guide, but I've heard from many others that it's been helpful for them along their recovery journey.

Let's dive in.

HONESTY & ROOT FEELINGS

When I was first enrolled in an inpatient eating disorder treatment program at a hospital, two vital statements were presented to me:

1. "If you can't be honest with yourself, you won't recover."
2. "The eating disorder is only a Band-Aid for what's underneath."

LIAR, LIAR, PANTS ON FIRE

One of the things I hated most about my eating disorder was that it turned me into a liar. My energy was spent abiding by my disorder's relentless commands and attempting to keep my secret world hidden. Every day was an exhausting slog through people, and food, and my rigid routines that had to be done or else my anxiety would thrash like a fish in the open air.

An eating disorder is an abuser. It gets its power from isolating us, and making us feel like it's our only friend, our lover, our god, our oxygen, our everything, until our worth depends on pleasing its destructive voice.

Eating disorders are the secret that will kill us. They rob us of our lives, our joy, our relationships, and connection, to name just a few things. They abuse us and make us lie for them. And we do it as long as we're keeping their secret.

The power of secrets is in their silence. Every lie we tell to protect our eating disorder allows it to gain power over our life.

It's difficult to sit with uncomfortable emotions. This is why we used the eating disorder in the first place – to distract us from them.

Two companion emotions that often come with eating disorders are **depression** and **anxiety**.

When I was anorexic, anxiety constantly pumped through my veins. When I switched over to bulimia, I sank into a black hole of depression. The two became co-existing destructive friends.

THE PERFECTIONIST AND THE FUCK YOU

The Perfectionist (anorexia/anxiety) moved like ants crawling through my veins, like an itch I couldn't scratch. I believed that if I just listened to the eating disorder and did everything she said, like a good little girl, I'd be happy and thin and powerful and all the other things she promised me. So, I complied. I hid her. I lied for her. I hollowed myself out to make a home for her. But she was never planning to grant her promises. She was a liar.

The Fuck You (bulimia/depression). We can only tell ourselves horrible things for so long before we rebel. After a time of trying to be perfect and failing daily, I was tired of being the good little girl. I hated the person the eating disorder had made me become. I felt like I'd been tricked and lied to. I was full of rage.

I was a "good little girl" who didn't know how to express negative emotions in a healthy way. If you'd asked me if I was angry, I would have told you no, because for years, I didn't think I was angry.

But at the hospital, during an Anger Wall exercise, a redheaded therapist revealed that *depression is rage turned inwards.*

Depression happens when we aren't allowed to feel rage, or to express anger, so we learn to turn it inwards on ourselves.

For years I told myself I wasn't angry. After all, I was a good little girl who smiled brightly and pushed away or played hide (without the seek) with her feelings. It didn't matter if I was rotting on the inside as long as I was thin and pretty on the outside.

When I was finally able to scratch through to the anger, I found that I was furious, filled and seething with rage. But I didn't have a voice, or a safe way to express my anger, because I was supposed to be the good girl. Now it ran through my body like an open floodgate, sloshing through my veins, screaming the names and places and memories it had kept during captivity. Hate is a strong word, but I felt it in my cells, towards myself, the eating disorder, God, family, friends, and strangers. It opened a hole in my chest and the darkness pooled in.

I'd been afraid of expressing my anger, of standing up for myself, of not knowing how, or not being strong enough, or enough of something. I was afraid that if I opened that hole in my chest, the black water would drown me.

In fact, the opposite happened. The more I was able to touch the raw and honest parts of my rage *and express it*, the rage I once feared actually became my ally, and began to dissipate.

It's like a monster under the bed. The story we make around the monster is much scarier than the pair of shoes it usually turns out to be. And if it turns out there are monsters under your bed, hiding under the covers doesn't make them go away.

Expressing the raw, honest, and rageful parts of myself eventually gave way to sadness and tears, and then there was space for peace. The creation of space for something else comes from getting in touch with what's under the eating disorder. What's the monster under your bed?

The Perfectionist (my anorexia) symbolized my desire for purity. The Fuck You (my bulimia) was a violent lashing out in rebellion. My therapist said, "You don't just rebel. You FU rebel."

I didn't have a voice with my anorexia, so it's quite fitting that I used an explosion of food in my bulimia as an attempt to say something I still couldn't voice.

HONESTY FOR RECOVERY

If we're being honest with ourselves, the disorder has stolen a part of our voice. Instead of sitting with uncomfortable feelings or being able to express them in a healthy way, we take the immediate path of our eating disorder. The eating disorder becomes a Band-Aid for everything we aren't able to feel or express in a healthy way.

The question is, *what are you hiding?*

The next time you're triggered and find yourself wanting to go down the eating disorder path, just take one minute to figure out what took place. What root issue just got triggered?

- If you were having a conversation with your mom, did it bring up feeling trapped or spoken over? Not having a strong voice of your own?
- If you were having a conversation with a friend, did it bring up feelings of insecurity around your worth, your looks, or your popularity/friendships?
- If you were having a conversation with a co-worker, did it bring up feelings of self-doubt, money insecurity, or being able to make it in the world on your own?

There are thousands of possibilities. Take 60 seconds to figure out the root issue that was triggered for you. Write it down. Then sometimes, you'll go ahead and do the eating disorder behavior.

(I know I'm not supposed to say that because it's dangerous and something we're trying to stop. I also know the truth is that we're going to do whatever we're going to do. In the beginning, we'll probably continue to do the behavior until we gain more clarity. So to be clear, I'm not advocating doing the behavior, nor am I giving permission. If you can avoid it, excellent. If you find yourself compelled, know that there's a lesson in each misstep. Be willing to learn it and adjust so that one day you'll be free).

Recovery isn't perfect, nor do you have to be. When you begin recovery, you're still going to want to throw up, or binge, or exercise, or whatever it is you do.

The important thing is this: FIRST write down the triggering event. If you follow the triggering event it will lead you to the root issue. However, all that's important right now is to identify the triggering event. THEN you may find yourself going to do the behavior. Later, you'll be able to resist the urge to do the eating disorder pattern, but at the beginning the goal is simply to gather information about yourself. Stopping and writing it down is powerful, because it interrupts the cycle of just going from stimulus to response. It creates a small space of awareness, like a breath, which is where health lives.

The first step in recovery is connecting the dots. If we're going to change our behavior, we must know *what happens within us* when we suddenly have the desire to self-soothe with the eating disorder.

Awareness is, essentially, us being honest with ourselves. And if we can be honest with ourselves, we can – and will – recover.

DISCUSSION QUESTIONS:

1. What do you dislike/hate most about your eating disorder? How have you felt tricked or lied to by it?
2. How would you describe your current relationship with your eating disorder? Is there anything good about it?
3. What emotions does the eating disorder help you hide from? What are you afraid would happen if you felt/expressed these emotions?
4. If your eating disorder were gone right now, how would your life immediately be different?

ACTION STEPS:

1. This week, every time you feel the urge to act on an eating disordered behavior, take a moment to write down the trigger event. At a more peaceful time, or with a safe person/licensed therapist, go through these triggers and see if you can identify the root issue that caused your spiral.

2
HOPE

PROMISES LINE THE CIRCLE OF SUFFERING

Those who've experienced a behavioral or substance addiction know the danger of making promises. We know the heartbreak that comes when we go to war with ourselves. We break promises, then feel like a liar and a failure.

There's only so long we can withstand our own abuse and self-loathing before defense mechanisms kick in. We then become non-committal and avoid making any promises at all. This appears to be the safe, logical route, because if we don't commit or promise anything, then we can't disappoint ourselves or anyone else.

Our culture however, rewards goal-setting, the mapping of steps, and pushing towards a time-framed accomplishment.

Even writing the sentence above produces an awful feeling in my body, full of dread and reminiscent of my eating disordered past. Time-lines or specific goal-setting feels a lot like promising, and my track record with promises normally went like this:

> *Make promise in attempt to get my act together. Feel good about self for a moment. Have lots of anxiety about keeping the promise. Inevitably break promise. Feel like a stupid, worthless, lying failure. Hate self. Wade in depression. Want to die ... Make promise. Etc.*

I'm intimately familiar with that circle of suffering, so I'm *not* going to ask you to make any promises.

What I will ask you to do, as we begin this recovery guide, is to *set a positive intention*.

There's some part of you, however small, that wants to recover from your eating disorder. If not, you wouldn't be reading this book. The issue is that there's probably another, larger part of you that doesn't know how to get there.

We're constantly told that in order to progress, we need a goal and a map for how we're going to get there. But we get stuck because if it's something we've never done before, we don't know *how* to do it.

Not knowing how to recover kept me sick for years. It allowed Lillie, my eating disorder, to feed me this particular lie:

"You don't how, so you can't move forward towards recovery."

The truth is, you don't need to know how. You just need to know where you'd like to be.

SETTING YOUR POSITIVE INTENTION

Imagine you're standing on a sidewalk. In front of you is a jam-packed, six-lane highway, the traffic zooming by at a frightening pace. On the far side of the highway is another version of you, holding a sugar cone with a bright, pink scoop of ice cream.

This is you, recovered.

In order to eat the pink ice cream cone, you have to get through the six lanes of wild traffic. But there's no break in the cars zooming by. There's no safe way to cross. You have no idea how you're going to get to the other side.

But you *know* that pink ice cream cone is yours. It has your name written all over it. And here's the trick: You don't have to know how you're going to cross the lanes of traffic. *You just have to acknowledge that you want to get there.*

For me, my pink ice cream cone was *freedom* and *happiness*. I wanted to be *free* of my mind's negative voices around food, and I wanted to feel *happy* when I ate.

My pink ice cream cone was a future vision of a dinner in Italy. It was dark outside as I sat at a circular, wooden table with a group of my closest friends. White Christmas lights glowed from the corner of the cozy room, and the table was laden with plates of delicious food and drink. But it was different than my reality at the time. Why? Because I wasn't unintentionally tracking how much everyone had eaten. I wasn't sure of what was on my plate, what I'd eaten or drunk. There was no second dialogue in my head and I had no idea where the bathroom was.

Instead, I was focused on the conversation, consumed and held in the presence of my friends. We were laughing wide, open-mouthed laughter that made our bellies hurt and tears well in our eyes. I was with those who loved me, who shared memories, stories, and lives. I was connected, accepted, at ease. Life was beautiful bliss and my heart was alive, expansive and free. There was no place I'd rather be.

What's your ice cream cone?

Maybe nothing comes to mind right away. If that's the case, keep the image of a pink ice cream cone until you can fill it in with something that works for you. If ice cream triggers you, replace it. What else do you enjoy in a healthy or symbolic way? Maybe you're standing across the highway holding a Christmas decoration, or plane tickets to Tahiti. Maybe there's a dinner table and you're laughing while eating with friends.

Let your intuition guide you. You'll know when the right image comes to you, because it will feel good. Healthy. Safe. Use whatever image inspires you; just make sure it's as solid and clear as a pink ice cream cone.

WHY THIS WORKS

The reason intention-setting is so powerful is that it activates a different part of ourselves. It skips over the anxiety-ridden, trying-to-figure-it-out brain, allowing us to access something higher.

Einstein once said, "No problem can be solved from the same level of consciousness that created it." That's basically what we're doing when we do this. By setting an intention, and holding a vision of where we want to be, we line up invisible resources, both within and outside of ourselves, that help us get there.

I don't know the precise science behind how this works (though research is being conducted on it), I just know that it does. It's like electricity: We don't have to know how it works to use it. We trust that if we flick on the light switch, our light will turn on. We trust this because we've seen it happen, repeatedly.

When you see your intentions happen in reality, you'll trust it, but let's take a leap and trust anyway, before we see them come to pass.

To wrap up, remember: You're not making any promises about the pink ice cream cone. You're simply saying, "Yep, pink ice cream cone, you look yummy. I'm not sure how I'm going to cross the highway to get to you, but one day I intend to be there."

Once you have your pink ice cream cone of intention, the part of you that wants to recover is ready to begin.

Congratulations. You're on your recovery path.

DISCUSSION QUESTIONS:

1. Have promises helped or hindered in your recovery? Explain.
2. How does *setting an intention* feel different than *making a promise*?
3. What is your pink ice cream cone of recovery?

ACTION STEPS:

1. Draw or write something on an index card that represents your version of the pink ice cream cone. Tape it to your bathroom mirror or somewhere you'll see it every day.

3

CHOICE

FORMULA FOR SUFFERING: "I CAN'T/I HAVE TO."

Living with disordered eating can make choice feel like a far-off notion, an item on a wish list.

My therapist once told me **I always had a choice**. But it didn't feel that way when I reacted in animalistic ways and fell into familiar patterns with ease. She used the example of traveling: "I could go to Paris," she said, "but I choose to stay home and pay my mortgage."

My brain heard, "I CAN'T go to Paris because I HAVE TO stay home and pay my mortgage."

What followed was a slew of crappy feelings about being trapped in a job and not being able to do something I wanted.

The truth is, we CAN do the things we want to do, but there are often consequences that stop us.

For example, in my past if I decided to go and gallivant around Italy, there were a number of possible side effects. I was married, working, in school for a master's degree in psychology, in rehearsal for a play, writing this recovery guide, and had a certain amount of money in my bank account. If I up and left, there'd be a number of consequences, many of which I'd classify as "problems."

Yes, it's one of my dreams to live in Italy. But I'm not upset that I'm not there. I know I have a choice as to where I live and what I do, and my life supports my priorities. I valued marriage, school, and my acting and writing work. Therefore, I chose to be present in my current life and marriage.

When I was in recovery, my therapist pointed out that I had a lot of internal "CAN'Ts." I had a whole list of excuses and negative mindsets around why I couldn't have the things I wanted.

How many times a day do you tell yourself the following?:

"Oh, I can't do X,Y, or Z …"
"That won't work because …"
"That sounds great, but …"
"I'd like that, but I have to …"

People have a fantastic knack for finding the negative. Our mind fixates on the one dot of black pepper on the otherwise spotless white wall. We brush away positive potential for many reasons, but mostly out of fear.

Fear keeps us stuck. It tells us we CAN'T, so we avoid stepping forward.

A few other versions of this dangerous word (CAN'T) are:

- I must …
- I have to …
- I'm obligated to …
- It's not possible to …
- I won't …
- It stresses me out to …
- I'm scared of …

For example, let's take an event like a binge and purge. When the event is over, it has already happened and thus lies in the past.

Yet we keep it alive by reliving it and playing it out in a loop in our minds. We drag past events into our present.

The event is just an event. It doesn't have meaning in and of itself. We *assign* meaning and energy to it, such as, "I failed," "I'm a bad person," "I'm never going to recover," etc.

The binge and purge itself said none of these things. We created these beliefs and then attached them to the event. When we play back the binge and purge in our mind, it's now full of those negative beliefs. These negative beliefs don't make us feel good, so we reach for our self-soothing tool, which is binging and purging, and thus the cycle continues.

Until we can consistently choose healthy patterns for ourselves, it's important to explore the choices we have *after* we've binged and purged and are feeling pretty crappy. Instead of berating ourselves with hateful words and sinking into a black hole of depression, we could say:

- "Yes, I binged and purged. AND I can now choose to go for a walk."
- "I choose to accept this is where I am right now, and I choose to love myself in this moment, anyway."
- "I choose to see the binge and purge as the only way I currently know how to soothe and take care of myself. I will figure out other ways, but for now, I choose not to judge myself for feeling overwhelmed and needing to take care of myself."

CHOOSING MORE CONSCIOUSLY

Choice is a part of daily life, yet we often feel trapped and confined by things we, "have to" do.

Let's look at school, because it's something we're all required to do.

The thought process of choosing school might look like, "Yes, I could make the choice to not go to school today. What would the consequences be? What would happen?" We might list consequences like getting grounded or suspended, falling behind on schoolwork, or even getting expelled. Then thoughts could go to, "That would suck ... I choose to go to school." Not "I HAVE to go to school," but "I *choose* to go to school."

You may choose to do something because it's better than the consequences of not. The point is, we *do* get to choose. I've found that the amount I suffer is directly related to how much choice I perceive I have. When I feel like I have no choice, I suffer tremendously.

As a young adult, I felt powerless a lot, because I didn't comprehend that I could make a different choice. The truth is, we *could* choose to walk out of our math class at any time and go off-campus. We could choose to go get coffee or a smoothie, or lie in a grassy field and look at the sky. But what would the consequences be? We might not *want* those consequences, so now it becomes a choice to go to English class, instead of choosing to ditch.

A more serious example: Say you're a teenage girl who is being molested by your stepfather. You could make the choice to run away from home. You could, but it would be difficult and very dangerous (especially if you're going to live on the street). AND you could still choose to do it.

You could also choose to continue living at home but get help via RAINN (the Rape & Incest National Network), which allows you to instant message with a counselor; it's free, secure, and confidential. You could also choose to read a book at the library about sexual abuse, and learn more about how you're not alone. Millions of people suffer from the horrible reality of being sexually abused.

The point is, you're in a horrific situation, and you still have choice. Holding onto our choices is what keeps us hopeful, resistant, and empowered.

CHOOSING YOUR INTERNAL REALITY

When we know we are at choice, we know we have power. We can't always control outside circumstances, but we always have the power to choose our internal reality.

We can begin by choosing words that will empower us. Phrases like:

- I can …
- I will …
- I'm excited for …
- I choose to …
- I want to …
- It brings me joy to …

By now, hopefully you're seeing that we can continue to feel powerless or we can choose to feel powerful. The energy around the words, "I can't" feels powerless and helpless, as though there's nothing we can do. In contrast, when we feel as though we're choosing to do something, our bodies and minds relax. Another option has been created, and we're not trapped. We've become powerful.

Life coach Christina Berkley has a powerful story of how she maintained her sanity during a sexual assault. Her mantra became, "What's the most powerful choice I can make right now?" Eventually it meant extricating herself from the situation, but until then, sometimes it just meant moving her arm in a certain way.

Her mantra helped her to realize she still had power. She was not completely helpless. She could still make some, tiny choices. She was still there.

Our internal sense of power is a vital locus. Helplessness and powerlessness are two of the lowest vibrational states, and human emotions. We all want to feel powerful. Recognizing and claiming our ability to choose helps us regain our power.

DISCUSSION QUESTIONS:

1. Name one small area in your life today that feels like the "I CAN'T go to Paris because I HAVE TO pay my mortgage" formula. Or, "I can't eat normally because I'll gain weight." What side effects do you experience when you think in the CAN'T/HAVE TO way?
2. What would happen if you "went to Paris" in your example? What are the potential consequences of your Paris trip? What are the possible perks?
3. What specific meanings or beliefs do you assign to your eating disordered behaviors? How might this contribute to keeping you in the eating disorder cycle?

4. What's your go-to danger word or phrase? (Danger words/phrases: I can't, I must, I have to, I'm obligated to, it's not possible to, I won't, it stresses me out to, I'm scared of, etc.)
5. How might recovery be different if you believed you always had a choice?

ACTION STEPS:

1. Write this list down on an index card and tape it to the bathroom mirror, keep it in your pocket, or set it as your phone's wallpaper:
   - I can …
   - I will …
   - I'm excited for …
   - I choose to …
   - I want to …
   - It brings me joy to …

Whenever you catch yourself saying any of the danger words, immediately replace it with any of the alternatives from the list, and repeat the sentence.

4

WANTS & DON'T WANTS

THINGS WE DON'T WANT

Most of us are pros at identifying the things we don't want. For example, "I don't want to feel controlled by the eating disorder."

It's more difficult to identify and state our wants.

Let's pretend the things we want are located in the neon green bull's-eye of a target. Let's also pretend we haven't told anyone that that's where our desires live. Only *we* can see the bull's-eye.

The people who love us, including our friends, family, and partners, try to give us what they think we want. They stand in the room, throwing darts around randomly at the wall, while we complain, "Ugh. Not there. I don't like that. Stop throwing the dart there."

The more darts they throw, the more upset we become, because we're not getting what we want. Because they love us and see we're frustrated, they continue to throw darts, desperately hoping to hit on something that will make us happy. The whole situation is silly and exhausting, because we're playing a game without having established any rules.

In order to actually get what I want, I must first know that the neon green bull's-eye on the target is where I want people to aim. This means I must *identify* what I want. Then, I must clearly *communicate* that I'd like people's darts to land in the neon green circle.

It all starts by rephrasing negatives.

REPHRASING NEGATIVES

Say I notice I get frustrated in conversations with my friend Jane, because I feel she controls the conversation and rarely asks about my life. I might leave a conversation with her thinking, *"I hate it when Jane over-talks. It's so irritating when she monopolizes the conversation. She doesn't ask me questions and doesn't care about me. She never listens."*

Great! We've just established a great negative list of things I *don't* want. Now, what *do* I want?

Maybe I want friendships that have equal sharing time. Maybe I want Jane to be interested in my life and ask follow-up questions. Maybe I want to be deeply listened to, and feel as though the other person hears me.

One way to twist a negative "don't want" into a positive "want" is by asking a simple question:

"If this wasn't happening, what could be happening instead?" or, "**What do I want instead?**"

Here's an example of a self-dialogue around the frustration with Jane. For clarity, I'll make it a conversation between person A and person Z (both exist within me):

REPHRASING EXAMPLE

A: I'm pissed because Jane doesn't listen to me!
Z: So if I weren't pissed, what would I be feeling instead, and what would be happening in the conversation? aka, What do I want instead?
A: Well, if I wasn't pissed, I'd want to feel heard, which would mean Jane wouldn't be trying to interrupt me and give me advice.
Z: What would Jane be doing instead?
A: She'd be listening to me.
Z: How would I know she's listening?
A: She wouldn't interrupt or give advice.
Z: What would she be doing instead?
A: Showing she's interested by looking at me. Waiting til I finish my thoughts

to respond and asking a pertinent follow-up question, like how I feel about the situation.

Z: Great!

By following the exercise above, you can pin down what you want – *identify* it. The next step is being able to clearly articulate and share your wants.

SHARING YOUR WANTS

We can only control ourselves. As much as we'd like to, we can't change others. Therefore, we can't control or change Jane's behavior. We can, however, *identify* our wants and *share* them with Jane.

Ex. "Hi Jane, I'd like to tell you about a situation that happened at work today, and it would feel really nice if you could just listen. I'm not looking for advice right now, but I'd love it if you asked me how I felt after sharing."

Knowing what we want (identifying our neon green bull's-eye) is a vital part of learning to advocate for ourselves. When we're clear on what we want, it's easier to get our wants and needs met. It also makes it possible to set boundaries, which is a crucial skill when it comes to recovery.

DISCUSSION QUESTIONS:

1. Share an example of a time when a loved one kept throwing darts but completely missed the bull's-eye. What were your reasons for keeping the bull's-eye a secret? How might the event have played out differently if you'd have told the person about the target?
2. Name a handful of things you *don't* want in your life (in relation to your eating disorder or your relationships). Then pair up with a group member, one person as A and one person as Z. Take turns going through the rephrasing exercise with each item on your list until you discover what you actually want.

3. Once you identify your wants, practice sharing them aloud with each member of the group. Each member of the group may respond with, "Thank you for sharing."

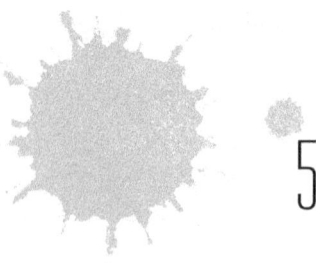

5

BOUNDARIES & SELF-ADVOCATING

BOUNDARIES. YES, THEY'RE AWESOME AND YOU WANT THEM.

Boundaries are by far the most important discovery of my early 20s. Even if you grew up with a loving family and have happy childhood memories, your family boundaries could have been dysfunctional or taught in dysfunctional ways.

Boundaries allow us to peacefully advocate for ourselves. Basically, having healthy boundaries means we can say YES when we *want* to do something, and NO when we *don't want* to do something (and not feel bad about our no).

I recall the first time boundaries came into my awareness. I was at the eating disorder hospital for inpatient treatment. The first week there, I frequently sat at the little yellow, public payphones in the hallway and pretended to be at home, as I called my mom and dad. I would speak and then cover the mouthpiece so that no background noise from the hospital would seep through. I lied about having a cold when my dad said I sounded stuffed up. I hadn't yet called my best friend, because I had no idea how to tell her that I was in the hospital because I threw up food and didn't want to be fat.

When I came back to the other hospital, girls they told me that I could only tell people what I wanted to. I didn't have to tell them everything. One girl said that I could tell them that, "I have an unhealthy relationship with food and I'm choosing to get some support around it." She paused, "You don't ever have to say the words 'I have an eating disorder.'" This blew me away. As they continued to talk about this magical word called "boundaries," I wrote the word in my journal to look up later. At that time, I had no idea what they were or how to implement boundaries in my life without severe anxiety and guilt.

A boundary is not an impenetrable fortress wall that keeps you separate from everyone else. A boundary is like a drawbridge around your castle, with a lever so you can open the doors. You are solely responsible for your castle. You're not responsible for your neighbor's castle, just as the neighbor is not responsible for your castle.

The drawbridge in your castle wall allows you choice. You can drop the bridge and let people into your space, or you pull up the bridge to keep people at a distance. This ability to open and retract your bridge can keep you emotionally and sometimes even physically safe.

We first practice boundaries with our words.

Even when we've identified our wants, we don't have to share them with another person unless we choose to. Equally, we are at choice about establishing a boundary: speaking up about something we *don't* want. For example:

- "I don't appreciate/it feels bad when you make comments about my body. I'd like it to stop."
- "It feels bad to me when I hear comments like that about my willingness to recover."
- "I appreciate the question, and I'm not comfortable talking about that right now. Thanks for understanding."
- "No. What you just did (that behavior) was not okay. I won't participate."

Boundaries help us establish where we begin and where we end, what we allow and what we don't. Setting clear boundaries is vital to our emotional safety. It also allows others to feel safe with us, because we've established the conduct of our castle.

As you recover and begin to learn and set boundaries, there will be pushback. Internally, there are your own "cant's." Externally, others might not like that you've established boundaries; setting them often changes the dynamic of the relationship. They may feel threatened. They used to be able to show up at your castle whenever the heck they wanted, drink your coffee, borrow horses, and fly kites off the roof — but now you've constructed a drawbridge. It doesn't mean you don't want them to visit. It means that you now have a say in terms of the visitation. Change is uncomfortable and that's okay.

Setting boundaries will help you have more energy, emotional freedom, better relationships, and greater self-esteem and personal power.

Saying NO is powerful. It makes it clear to us, and others, that people can't do whatever they want to us, or with us.

As you begin to set boundaries, uncomfortable emotions pop up, such as shame, guilt, and fear. You may even have people suddenly tell you, "You are so selfish!"

BEING SELFISH

"Selfish" is a little word that holds a lot of negative charge. It causes discomfort. Often we give in to what another person wants just so we're not labeled "selfish." Many times, the word is used to manipulate people.

I love the word selfish. In fact, I proudly claim that, "Yes, I am selfish."

Why? Because I choose to take care of my needs so I can help others from the overflow. In this way, I can help from joy, and not from resentment or obligation.

"Selfish" is a word people have tried to dirty with their shame and guilt. For me, being selfish means I listen to myself, acknowledge my needs, and take care of myself with kindness. Yes, please. Sign me up for that selfishness.

If the word "selfish" triggers you, challenge it. What positive things could "selfish" mean for you as you move forward into recovery?

HELPING OTHERS

Most people with eating disorders are intelligent and deeply caring. We go above and beyond to meet the needs of other people. Although being caring and of service are fantastic things, people can unintentionally take advantage of our soft hearts. We can find ourselves in situations where we're helping at the expense of ourselves. We may not want to help anymore but don't know how to say no, feel bad about saying no, or are guilt-tripped when we try to back away. Eventually, our helping hearts can become burdened with the obligation of helping instead of with the joy of helping.

If you're no longer helping from a place of joy, stop. Learn to empower instead.

EMPOWERING YOURSELF AND OTHERS

When you have clear boundaries, you allow others to reap the natural consequences of their behavior without feeling guilt or anxiety.

When we step in and fix someone else's problem, we take their power away. It's akin to ripping open a caterpillar's cocoon or cracking an egg to assist the baby bird into the world.

If we were to do these things in nature, the butterfly and the chick would die. Their act of struggling propels them into the world — by pushing blood into their wings. It makes their wings strong enough to fly. People operate best when they have their sense of personal power intact. Allow them to "suffer" and work through their discomfort for their benefit. It's not cruelty; it's kindness.

Support others by listening, empathizing, encouraging, and holding a safe space for them to share. But let them do their own work and go through their process. We each have our own cocoons and eggshells to emerge from. Focus on your own.

HURTING PEOPLE'S FEELINGS

As you continue setting boundaries, there are times when you'll feel bad about "hurting someone's feelings." This situation plays out even with people we don't know.

For example, you go to a restaurant because you're in the mood for their fluffy pancakes. When the pancakes come, they're flat like crepes, and taste as though the griddle wasn't cleaned between meal prep. It would be easy to send the pancakes back, right?

For many of us, it's not, because we construct stories around these events. We might think, "Oh no, if I send the pancakes back the staff might be mad or irritated with me. I might hurt the cook's feelings. It might reflect badly on the restaurant. They might think I'm a bitch."

Yes, all of these things are possible. However, you're not telling grandma, who toiled in the kitchen all morning, that you think her personal pancakes suck. You're at a business establishment and are not satisfied with their advertised product. It's not personal. It's a business transaction.

Also, any possible responses from the staff at the restaurant are not your responsibility or concern. Your part is to do your best to be kind and loving when you tell the waitress you're not satisfied with your pancakes. *Other people's responses are not your responsibility.* They're allowed to have their feelings, even if they vastly differ from yours.

THE BEST PEOPLE IN YOUR LIFE

One day on my recovery path, I realized the importance of having people in my life with whom I could speak honestly, and lovingly. Walking on eggshells is exhausting, and who wants a floor covered in broken eggshells?

Relationships are constantly being shaped. As I explored setting boundaries, some relationships grew closer, and some grew apart. The people in my current circle can handle me speaking my truth with love. If something doesn't feel right or there's a conflict, I can talk about it with them without the terror that I'm going to lose their love or friendship.

It feels wonderful to be supported in this way. Each step you take towards your own boundary-setting is a step towards positive relationships with yourself and others.

THE PENDULUM SWING

In the process of developing and setting boundaries, you may notice you swing from one side of the pendulum to the other. Everything you said "Yes" to in the past, may now be a firm and even angry "No."

This is OK. The pendulum swing reminds you that in the past, you spent a lot of time not listening or taking care of yourself first. That's also OK. You probably weren't taught how to do so. The important thing is that now, you're learning to listen and take care of yourself.

As you continue to set boundaries, you'll experience greater emotional safety. Then you'll find yourself somewhere in the middle of the two extremes. Boundaries become fun and peaceful.

And one day, you'll let down and take up your drawbridge without even thinking about it.

DISCUSSION QUESTIONS:

1. Describe your relationship to the word "selfish." How does it make you feel to be called "selfish?"
2. Share a time when you wanted to say/do something for yourself but didn't, out of fear and worry of hurting a person's feelings. If you could have responded without fear or worry, what would you have said?

HELPFUL READING:

- *Boundaries: When to Say Yes When to Say No to Take Control of Your Life*, by Dr. Henry Cloud and John Townsend
- *Boundaries Workbook: When to Say Yes When to Say No to Take Control of Your Life*, by Dr. Henry Cloud and John Townsend
- *Safe People: How to Find Relationships That Are Good for You and Avoid Those That Aren't*, by Dr. Henry Cloud and John Townsend

6

IS THIS TRUE?

ARE YOUR THOUGHTS TRUE?

One of my friends loves the "walk and talk." When I lived in Hawaii, we'd put on our sneakers, take long power walks under the bright blue sky, and chat about life.

I began to notice that while processing a topic, she'd ask me the same simple question:

"Is that true?" Then she'd wait for me to fumble my way through an explanation or excuse.

For example, I'd say, "My boss *hates* me."

She'd say, "Is that true?"

And I'd have to actually stop and consider the question. Did my boss actually hate me, or was there something else going on and that was just how I was perceiving the situation? *Was it true?*

Until my friendship with her, no one had ever directly asked me that question. (Or if they had, I'd never been asked it so often.) In the beginning, it caught me off guard. I routinely found myself confused and questioning my own logic. I was forced to justify things I'd always just taken at face value.

Then something magical happened. Answering that simple question over and over allowed me to see that many of the statements or thoughts I was blindly accepting as truth, actually weren't.

Some of my relentless eating-disordered thoughts included:

- *You're fat.*
- *You're worthless.*
- *You have no friends.*
- *You're weak.*
- *You're a failure.*
- *You're alone.*
- *You're disgusting.*
- *You can't trust yourself.*
- *You're worthless.* (This one came up a lot.)
- *You're a fat pig.*

Then there the times when I strung them all together, like making the pearl necklace from hell:

"You stupid, fat, worthless, pussy, bitch, baby, pathetic piece of shit. I hate you."

THE TRUTH ABOUT FAT

For almost everyone with an eating disorder, the idea that you're fat is a constant. It's ruthless, pervasive, and relentless. The belief that we're fat can drive us, rule us, and dominate us. If we let it, it can become our everything — our biggest fear and our biggest lie.

Because here's the question: *Is it true?*

One silly thing I've heard that stuck in my mind is:

"You have fat, but you're not fat."

When this was said to me I cringed, because I didn't want to have *any* fat. I didn't get the difference between the statement and despised the idea that any fat on my body even existed.

But the reality is that as human beings, we *need* some fat on our bodies.

WHY WE NEED FAT

Fat is essential. Our bodies absolutely must have it in order to be healthy and function properly.

Consider the following:

- Fat is the first fuel our bodies burn for energy, otherwise our muscles get eaten (which isn't a good look).
- Every cell in our body has a little fatty membrane around it. Without this, the cells can't function properly.
- Fat acts as an insulating sheath surrounding nerve fibers that carry important messages.
- Some vitamins, such A, D, E, and K, are fat-soluble vitamins, which means fat from foods helps our intestines absorb these vitamins into the body. In other words, without fat, it doesn't matter how much vitamin D we get — we literally can't take it in.
- Fat insulates us, helps regulate body temperature, and keeps our skin looking good. Without fatty acids, our skin becomes flakey and dry.
- Fats are the building blocks of important hormones that help regulate many of the body's functions, including the production of sex hormones.
- Most of our vital organs (especially the kidneys, heart, and intestines) are held in place and protected from injury by a layer of fat. This fat cushions our essential organs, and is so important that our bodies will burn it only as a very last resort.

If we aim to have no fat, we are essentially aiming to be dead.

THE FEAR OF FAT

I'm not a nutritionist, but I know that when we eat natural fats, such as avocado, coconut oil, or macadamia nuts, our body knows how to process them and to use them for our health. And they don't make us "fat."

There was a time, though, when I was afraid of all fat. There was no way in hell you'd get me to eat an avocado or a nut. At one point in my disorder, I became obsessed with fat-free ice cream. One day, on a family vacation, my aunt did the grocery shopping and happened to get the "wrong" type of ice cream. "Wrong" because the fat content on the carton said 0.5g of fat per serving instead of 0.0. I refused to eat any of it, my aunt had a fit, and it caused a family argument about me.

Looking back on it now, it seems silly. But at the time, the little fat content number dictated my "allowed" foods (foods I allowed myself to eat). The idea of fat also kept me from making memories with my family during the vacation, because I was preoccupied with the constant terror of how my food was being prepared.

Was I fat? No.
Did I think I was fat? Yes.
Did I ever question this notion? No.
Why not?

QUESTION EVERYTHING

My eating disorder had me believe everything "she" told me was absolute truth. If she said I was fat, then I was fat. If she said I was stupid, I was. If she said I was a complete failure, I'd prostrate myself and beg to be in her good graces again. I believed everything she said without question.

Since she'd stolen my voice, I didn't have a voice to challenge her anymore. I forgot how to argue, how to stand up for myself against the bully in my head, and how to hold my ground when I was assaulted with her words.

The magic of the question, "Is this true?" lies in its power to distance us from the negative voice of our disorder. When we can take that step back, even just for a moment, we begin to take our power back.

An eating disorder thrives off of us never questioning it, and then doing everything it says we have to do. But the moment we start to create space by asking a question like, "Is this true?", tiny fractures begin to form in the eating disorder's armor.

She's not invincible, although she does a stellar job of fooling us. The more we ask questions and challenge her faulty logic, the looser her grip on us becomes.

DEVELOPING DOUBT IN THE EATING DISORDER

My friend's question, while annoying at first, was actually a gift. Soon, it became an automatic response to the negative, cruel thoughts the eating disorder threw my way. She'd say something mean, and BAM!, the question would fire: "Is that true?" Suddenly, I was defending myself, going to battle on my own behalf.

When my eating disorder threw me, "You're disgustingly fat," the immediate response clicked in: "Is this true?"

While, yes, there were times I believed it *was* true, often there were other things that worked against it. Is it true? Well, do I have any evidence that it is? No … in fact, three different people have told me they're concerned about how thin I am. So, is it true? Maybe not. Actually, *probably* not.

Anything. One thing. Find it and build on it.

It might be the way people easily muscle you in basketball practice because you're an unhealthy kind of thin. It may take looking around at other people and realizing there are multiple shapes and sizes. It could be finding one person you admire who is your size or body shape. It can be anything as long as it places doubt on what the eating disorder is saying.

Each time we challenge the eating disorder with this question, finding more and more ways to prove her wrong, we create another crack. We start to expose the lies she tells us, lies we've perhaps *never* questioned before.

Today, when I look in the mirror, there's sometimes a small voice that says, "Uh oh, look at the cellulite on your ass and thighs. You're getting a little fatty." Then the immediate response kicks in – "Is this true?"

The answer is no. I'm not. I'm a normal human being, with a normal body. Sure, I have more fat around this area than I used to, but the price I used to pay for less fat there was very high. It was restricting, and brought with it unhealthy binging and purging, anxiety and depression, hopelessness, hiding, lies, secrets, shame, fear, powerlessness, self-loathing, sorrow, and isolation.

So: Am I fat? No.
Do I have fat? Yes.

And I'm OK with that, because the price I pay now is light and easy.

My life is joyful and fun. I laugh and smile. I can eat anything. I don't think about food. I like my body, appreciate it, even love it. I feel free. The dictator of my eating disorder is gone. I came back from war with my voice.

And it all started with one magic question:

Is this true?

DISCUSSION QUESTIONS:

1. What are a few of your relentless eating disordered thoughts?
2. What is your belief about foods with fat content? Are there foods you like but don't allow yourself to eat or enjoy because of their fat content?
3. Why is it important for the body to have some fat? Do you have any safe foods that are high in fat?
4. What price do you pay for your eating disorder? What specifically does it cost you and those around you?

ACTION STEPS:

1. This week, challenge each eating disordered thought by asking, "Is this true?" Come up with at least one possibility as to why the thought might not be true.

7

GOD

In high school, my favorite poem was *The Love Song of J. Alfred Prufrock* by T.S. Elliot. A few lines from it:

> "And I have known the eyes already, known them all —
> The eyes that fix you in a formulated phrase,
> And when I am formulated, sprawling on a pin,
> When I am pinned and wriggling on the wall,
> Then how should I begin
> To spit out all the butt-ends of my days and ways?
> And how should I presume?"

I identified with the bug, trapped and pinned like an insect specimen on the wall. I struggled daily, impaled on the sharp pin of my eating disorder. My arms and legs flailed. And all the while, God watched, and did nothing.

GOD WATCHED AND DID NOTHING

As a child, I grew up loving God, feeling as though He were a friend and protector. I saw Him as a superhero, doing things like saving Daniel from the mouth of the lions, parting the Red Sea, telling warriors how to win battles, and keeping Jonah alive for three days in the belly of whale.

As a child, I also grew an itching need to be the good girl, a desire to be chosen, and a story I created about earning my wings.

My problem with God started when I promised Him I'd stop my eating disorder. I'd lie on my carpet, crying for Him to make it stop, to take away the demons that had latched themselves to me and took pleasure in impaling me with their pins. I knew He wanted me to stop, but I was perpetually back at square one.

My God could save me with a single word, with a breath, but He didn't. What did that say about me? The story I told myself was that I was bad, worthless. The story said the very core of me was disgusting, dark, and putrid. After all, I routinely broke promises. I lied. I was a bad person.

The story said I wasn't good enough to be saved.

CHILDREN OF NEGLECT

The Christian God I was raised with was a parental figure. When children are neglected by the adults who are supposed to take care of them, they don't realize the neglect isn't about them.

Instead, children unconsciously blame themselves, assuming it's their fault. They think they must have done something wrong and that they're not good enough. It's easier for children to accept that they've done something wrong, because the alternative conclusion is that they're unlovable. How can a small child live under the weight of that burden?

After living with my eating disorder for years, I despised going to church because it rubbed my face in what a failure I'd become. The eating disorder itself came with constant shame and guilt. Then I'd go to church and be impaled again by God's watching. His disappointing eye caused even more guilt and shame to overwhelm me. I felt that if God wasn't helping me, it must be because I was bad, worthless, and unlovable.

How does someone with an eating disorder deal with negative emotions like guilt or shame?

Trick question. The answer is usually that we don't; instead, we use an eating disordered pattern to numb out. In my case, it was binging and purging.

It's a cycle. The disorder feeds the negative emotions, and the negative emotions trigger the disorder.

We are rats in a wheel, spinning but going nowhere.

ANGER AT GOD

If we believe God is there, it's heartbreaking to think He's just watching us squirm like an insect on a pin. I'd prayed to God to take away the eating disorder, to heal me, and to set me free. I'd begged, cried face down into my carpet, and been ignored. When we feel that an all-powerful God has chosen to ignore us, we experience the ache of worthlessness. Being ignored is worse than being told no. Being ignored makes us feels that we're not even worth the effort of a reply, as though we're nothing.

Ultimately, I realized that the deep internal cloud of sadness I experienced in church was masking my fiery anger at God.

It turned out that I was *furious* at this father figure. I saw Him as not only not protecting me from the worst of my life – the eating disorder itself – but of *knowing about it and doing nothing.*

It's one thing not to help someone if you don't know they're being wounded. But in my world, God was witnessing me suffer, and choosing to do nothing. In other words, it wasn't that He didn't know I was in pain; it was that He didn't care.

In my time at the hospital, during the Anger Wall exercise, the facilitator had us repeat these words: *"I have a right to my anger. My anger is valid."*

Then we threw clay against the wall, giving voice to our anger.

I was surprised to discover that once I got in touch with my anger, it wasn't my parents or my teachers or the people who told me I was too thin that I was most angry at — it was God. And I wasn't just mad, I was *enraged*.

A lot of us are angry at God. Maybe we're angry but were taught that we "couldn't" or "weren't allowed" to be angry at Him/Her – that it wasn't appropriate. Maybe we projected our feelings about our caregivers onto God, assuming S/He was just like our alcoholic father, or our depressed mother. This isn't conscious, but it's common.

Most times, there's an ocean of rage behind our sadness. Depression is often a front for anger. And many times, anger is a step forward. It gets us closer to the truth of how we're really feeling – especially if we weren't "allowed" to get angry in our family system.

Ultimately, we were all just children who were hurt or let down. The wounds were deep, but accessing them can bring us freedom.

Once you get in touch with your anger, here are some ways to express it safely:

- Talk it out with a safe person.
- Go to the ocean, a swimming pool, or even in your bathtub, and scream underwater.
- Get somatic therapy (bodywork therapy). See Chapter 18.
- Incorporate movement into your recovery, as unexpressed emotions often become trapped and stagnant in our bodies, leading to other physical ailments.
- Write an angry letter to God. Read it out loud to yourself or with a safe person. You may choose to tear it up after reading, or burn it.

SEEING GOD AS FRIEND, NOT FOE

In my journey, I went away from Christianity and came back to it later, with a different understanding of God.

I was originally taught a belief system created by people that unintentionally led me to believe God was disappointed in me. When I came back, I took with me the belief that God was love. I adjusted the way I viewed God, and that changed everything.

As adults, we can filter and rewrite our beliefs. We can choose to throw out things that no longer serve us, and embrace parts that bring us peace and joy.

We often do this by working through "negative" emotions (like anger), which allows us to see more clearly. Then we can choose what we want, instead of being unconsciously trapped in the emotion.

When I believed God was love, I began to embrace a world where God had been working things out, off the view of my radar screen. I began to see that people had come into my life at vital times to nudge me in the direction of my healing.

I began to see my suffering as a form of wisdom.

LESSONS CAN BE LEARNED THROUGH LOVE OR SUFFERING

We can learn lessons through love or through suffering. I'd personally like to learn all of mine through love, but the fact is, most of my important lessons have been gleaned through pain.

I'm someone who wants to analyze the miracle instead of just be healed. I need to know *why* and *how*, which is why if God had magically healed me it wouldn't have been fulfilling. (I also wouldn't be writing this right now if I hadn't gone through what I had, and I value being able to share my story.)

Yes, the suffering was painful, but the gratitude afterwards was immense.

WITHIN THE SICKNESS LIES THE CURE

I believe my lessons have been learned this way due to the homeopathic principle of "like cures like." This means that within the sickness lies the cure. If it can *cause* it, it can *cure* it.

Essentially, a homeopathic medicine works to gently exaggerate the "stuck" symptoms, to trigger a healing response. Pain is often the best way to pull up the roots of a core issue and expose where we need healing and homeostasis.

My eating disorder showed me all the ways I was stuck, and exposed the black holes in my own psycho-education – all the skills I needed to develop that I'd never learned or been taught. And ultimately, anger and hatred towards God was part of what guided me back to God's love.

If you're in a tumultuous place in your relationship with God, that's OK. You're allowed to be angry at God. God can handle your anger. You're allowed to work your own process, at your own pace.

Then you can come back on terms that bring you peace.

DISCUSSION QUESTIONS:

1. Do you identify with the bug pinned on the wall? If not, what image better fits your identity within your eating disorder?
2. Share your current view of, feelings, or relationship with God. How has your eating disordered altered this? Do you see God as friend, foe, or something else?
3. Would you say you're angry with/at God? Have you ever expressed this anger in any form? What's one safe way you could do this?
4. Do you believe your eating disorder can be a tool to illuminate ways you are stuck? Why/why not?
5. If you could have a connection with God that you felt good about, what might that look like?

ACTION STEPS:

1. This week, reflect on one lesson you've learned through suffering, and one you've learned through love. How did the learning experiences differ?
2. Throughout the week, pay attention to lessons (big or small) and how you learn. At the end of the week, jot down how you think you learn. Do you find yourself learning through suffering or love, pain or joy?

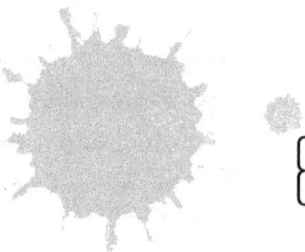

8

SEXUAL ABUSE & EATING DISORDERS

SEXUAL ABUSE AND ITS CONNECTION TO EATING DISORDERS

Not all people who have an eating disorder have experienced sexual abuse. However, there is a significant correlation between the two – the statistics are so dramatic that it would be negligent not to talk about it.

First, a few facts:

1. In the U.S., 28% of those aged 14 to 17 have been sexually victimized.
2. 40-60% of people who develop eating disorders have experienced sexual abuse.

This means roughly 1 in 3 or 4 adolescents are sexually abused, and that *almost half* of them will develop an eating disorder as a way to cope with the trauma.

You don't have to be touched to be sexually abused. Sexual abuse also consists of non-contact abuse, such as being forced to watch sexual acts, listen to sexual talk, view sexual parts of the body, or look at sexually-explicit material.

Other types of covert/no-touching abuse (non-contact abuse) including receiving inappropriate looks or comments as you develop during puberty. Someone could repeatedly walk in when you're undressed. They might subtlety watch you while you're naked, or position themselves where you might see them naked.

A large number of those who've experienced contact and/or non-contact sexual abuse develop eating disorders as a way to cope with overwhelming emotions like shame, confusion, worthlessness, anger, and fear.

Sexual abuse is a dramatic violation of boundaries. It teaches you that you don't have control over your own body. If someone can hurt you against your will, you naturally conclude that your body is not a safe place to be.

There are many reasons children don't tell if they're being sexually abused. They may not realize something is wrong, or don't want to believe something is wrong. Many times, they're dependent on the abuser (a caretaker or family member). They're often afraid to tell their parents out of fear of not being believed, or of getting in trouble (for some, the abuser *is* a parent). Many feel guilty and somehow think it's their fault. Even more confusing is that for some people, the sexual abuse is the only form of love or attention they receive.

Sexual abuse and eating disorders share common threads, such as debilitating shame and guilt. They both create a desire to numb out, rage, self-punish, self-soothe, and protect.

They share the common denominators of *shame* and *secrecy*.

Dealing with memories of past sexual abuse is painful. Victims can experience symptoms of **post-traumatic stress** (stress that keeps happening long after the actual traumatic event has occurred). If the victim experienced some form of pleasure from the abuse, guilt about this can keep a person in an eating disorder cycle as way to punish any sexual enjoyment. If the body is not a safe space to live, we naturally become disconnected from our internal cues with regard to sexuality and hunger, which leads to a number of issues.

Those who experience sexual abuse often cope by focusing on eating patterns and body image, using food as a way to stuff, starve, purge, or numb emotional wounds.

Some victims gain or lose weight in an effort to appear unattractive. Unconsciously, they believe manipulating their body size will help them avoid sexual advances or further abuse. For example, those who've gained weight as emotional padding can be terrified to lose it. Often the abuse occurred when the person was a child, so the weight can act as a protective device to help them from feeling small or childlike.

Others strive for perfect bodies as a way to gain control, an attempt to avoid ever feeling powerless or re-experiencing unwanted feelings.

HEALING FROM SEXUAL ABUSE AND EATING DISORDER FALLOUT

If you were sexually abused, the most important thing to remember is this: It was NOT your fault. It is NEVER your fault, no matter what. It doesn't matter whether you experienced some pleasure from it (if that's true for you). It is NOT and was NEVER your fault.

The first step in healing from sexual abuse is to tell someone you trust. Find a safe person and space to share the emotional and visceral pain. I recommend a licensed therapist who specializes in sexual abuse and trauma.

Secrets get their power from silence. Yes, sharing shines light on a wound, but it's also the first step to healing it.

As you begin to heal and grieve, you'll be sending messages to your body that it no longer needs to engage in disordered eating as a means to cope.

OWNING OUR BODIES

Both sexual abuse and eating disorders create an atmosphere of detachment from the body, because it wasn't a safe place to be.

The truth is that our bodies and our sexuality are ours, to have and to own.

We have a right to say that we don't want to be touched, don't want to participate, or don't like a certain behavior. We have a right to have our voice respected. As adults, we can remove ourselves from situations that are destructive. As adolescents, we can tell someone safe. We have a right to our own bodies and to express our sexuality in ways that we choose and agree to.

It is possible to heal from your past. You are not stuck, and you are not alone.

Our body is our home. Everything we do in this world will be done with, and in, this body.

We can heal and come home to a body that is a safe place in which to reside.

DISCUSSION QUESTIONS

1. What does the statement "My body is my home" mean to you? Do you see your body as a safe home? If not, what would allow you to feel safer in your body?
2. If someone were sexually abused, what are a few specific ways they could begin the healing process?
3. How are eating disorders and sexual abuse connected? What are some possible reasons that someone who has been abused would then develop an eating disorder?
4. What are some possible reasons someone might keep sexual abuse a secret?

ACTION STEPS:

1. The *Practice Receiving* exercise (individually). While standing in front of the mirror, say, "My body is my home." Gently touch a part of your body that triggers you. Lovingly say, "This body is my home." Each time, answer, "Thank you. I receive that."
2. Sharing a secret with someone safe is the first step to healing and taking your power back. If you've been sexually abused and/or it's resulted in an eating disorder, I encourage you to seek out a licensed therapist with a specialty in sexual abuse and/or trauma. If you're an adult, this week find 3-5 therapists and give them a call. See Chapter 17 for more details on how to do this. If you're a teen, make an appointment with one of your school counselors, contact the RAINN instant messaging service, or if it's safe (and possible), ask a parent to help you set up a therapy appointment.

9

BECOMING FRIENDS WITH THE FEMININE

PUBERTY AND STUNTED SEXUALITY

Puberty is a prime time for the development of eating disorders. Girls' bodies change shape, laying down fat on the hips and breasts, growing hair "down there," and periods begin.

This can be a strange and terrifying time. We can feel like the body is out of control, doing things we don't want, and we may start getting attention we might not be ready for or desire. I know I wasn't ready for any of these, nor did I want them.

Growing up, I identified as a tomboy. I was an athlete who was often the only girl on the boys' basketball team. I wore similar clothes to my brother, including white tank tops, and I liked when people asked if we were twins.

Then one day, I started to grow little Hershey Kiss buds on my chest. I couldn't wear tank tops anymore without drawing attention. It was like I suddenly had two arrows pointing out my difference, when all I wanted to do was fit in.

For a solid year, every night before I went to sleep, I prayed to God that I wouldn't grow boobs.

On my sports teams (which consisted almost entirely of boys), I was already different because I was a girl. But then I had to wear a mortifying *training bra* and was subjected to torturous period cramps.

Oh, joy, I was becoming a woman. But no one ever asked me if I wanted this, and I did not.

I hated everything about it.

Survival psychology says that we side with the "strongest" member of our family. If the strongest member is male, then we often grow up valuing masculine traits as powerful and worthy. The downside is that we can devalue or reject feminine traits, viewing them as weakness.

I experienced being a woman as something that made me an outcast. The transformation was out of my control, like Jekyll and Hyde, but I couldn't change back. I refused to accept becoming a woman, which I viewed as weakness.

So I did the next best thing (to subconsciously rebel): I took control by focusing on food, exercise, and the size of my body. At least I *thought* I was taking control back by becoming anorexic.

This rejection of the feminine lasted for a decade, until one day my therapist had me create a collage. On it were spirals, circles, and flow. She told me I was imbalanced, craving the feminine.

Eating disorders (especially anorexia) can stunt both our sexuality and our sexual development, keeping us in a childlike or androgynous body where we think we'll be safe or powerful.

Part of my anorexia was an attempt to make myself childlike again, when things were happier, when I fit in and felt strong, when I ran with the boys on equal footing.

For millions of girls and women suffering with eating disorders, part of the healing process involves becoming friends with our feminine power and learning to own our sexuality.

BECOMING FRIENDS WITH OUR FEMININE

In western society, feminine energy is seen as less valuable than masculine energy. For years I rejected the feminine because I believed it was weak.

The truth is, both energies are valuable. And they must be recognized equally in order for there to be balance.

Masculine energy encompasses striving, competition, determination, logic, rigidity, rationality, analysis. It's fearless, courageous, goal-oriented, and

loyal. Masculine energy comes from the left brain, which relies on math and science. In western society, we're taught to think in a masculine way, and to view this way as powerful and more desirable for success.

Feminine energy encompasses creativity, empathy, collaboration, compassion, and intuition. It comes from our right brain and offers us wisdom, patience, nurturing, and flexibility. When we're in our feminine energy, we receive, open, and flow.

All of us have both masculine and feminine energy.

When we have an eating disorder, most of the time one or both of these energies is severely out of balance. It can be wounded, misunderstood, disrespected, or forced into silence.

The rigidity of eating disorders stops our flow and disconnects us from receiving. We shut down. Often an imbalance of masculine energy in our eating disorder forces us to strive for the disorder's demands, but offers us no satisfaction, no nourishment or fulfillment.

Part of recovery involves coming back into balance, including recognizing and embracing both aspects of ourselves: the masculine and the feminine. One way to do this is to look up to role models that embody one or both aspects.

Many people grow up without strong feminine or masculine role models. That's OK. Role models can be found outside of your family of origin. Take a look at the people around you, on TV, or in books. Choose someone that embodies traits and a healthy character that you can look up to and to model yourself after.

For example, one of my role models for the healthy feminine today is Esther, from the Bible. She's assertive, not aggressive, and put her life on the line to save her people. She acted in a wise and conscious way, taking into account all parts of the situation. She knew when to hold information close and when to reveal it.

There are a few women in the acting industry that have also become my role models. Instead of still pining to play the 16-year-old, doe-eyed lead, these women are all older than I am. These actresses represent grace, power, self-assuredness, and are stunning in their beauty and strength — something I can value and embody at any age.

There are also a few select women writers and speakers that I adore for their humor, dedication to their research and art, freedom of spirit, and willingness to explore life in all its depth, change, chaos, and beauty.

DISCUSSION QUESTIONS

1. If you identify as female, what were your thoughts and reactions as your body "became a woman?" If you identify as male, what were your thoughts and reactions on your body "becoming a man?" Did puberty play a part in your eating disorder?
2. Who are your role models for feminine and masculine energy? Is there someone you admire that could serve as a healthy role model for you?
3. If you were to invite more feminine energy into your eating disorder recovery, what might that look like?

ACTION STEPS:

1. The Practice Receiving Exercise (individually). While standing in front of the mirror, say, "My body is my home." Gently touch a part of your body that triggers you. Lovingly say, "This body is my home." Each time answer, "Thank you. I receive that."
2. Create a drawing, painting, or collage of your masculine and feminine energy represented together on the page in a way that feels peaceful and balanced.

10

MODELS & THE MEDIA

AN ODE TO MY FORMER DREAM

When I was in my teens, I wanted to be a runway model. I flipped through magazines and watched the catwalk on TV, viewing models as people who had the kind of power I wanted: the ability to claim and hold all the eyes in the room without uttering a single word.

In high school, I had zero skills to defend myself against catty girls. Since I couldn't be mean, I was an easy target for teasing. It was "all in fun," of course, but it wasn't fun for me.

I lived with the naive belief that if was skinny like the runaway models, I'd be strong. No one would dare tease me. I'd be the girl who could look at you sideways and stop your conversation mid-word, your mouth hanging open. I'd be like the models on stage who sashayed their hips in rhythm, black eyes dusty, heroin chic, clothes falling straight down.

I didn't notice that models don't talk. They're paid to balance beautifully on high heels, look gorgeous, and shut the hell up. No one peruses the catwalk or indulges a magazine and wonders what the girls are thinking. Girls are pretty hangers for clothes, furniture that sells a rug, images that teens (like me) used to measure themselves in the world, standards by which young men are also taught to judge.

I spent countless hours looking at magazines wondering why I didn't look like that, wondering how I could look like that. Obsession isn't just for Calvin

Klein. But it was modeled by Kate Moss, who once said, "Nothing tastes as good as skinny feels."

What is that supposed to teach me when I'm sweet 16?

THE MEDIA'S IDEA OF SKINNY

The "in" body shape for models has drastically changed since the late 80s and early 90s, when Cindy Crawford, Linda Evangelista, and Naomi Campbell were household names. Models today are stick thin and look like they might fall over if you blew a heavy breath their way.

Very few women are naturally the size and shape of a supermodel. Even professional models must diet to the point of starving themselves to keep up with ever-thinner standards. Designers make clothes that will fall off the model's body. The problem is that their ideal is a six-foot woman with the body of a young boy.

In order to work in the industry, girls diet, starve, or have breast reductions. They faint often, and have been known to use cotton balls or tissue to fill their empty stomachs. Some photo shoots involve a model lying down in a demure pose, or resting against furniture. When we see those photos in magazines, we have no idea that sometimes the model was too weak to stand up.

If you do a simple Google image search for runway models, you'll notice they're all extremely tall and thin. In my teens, when I had my eating disorder, I had pictures of extremely thin models taped on my wall as motivation. Back then, I thought their bodies were ideal.

But beyond that exoskeleton and that one flashbulb moment in time, most of these models use their precious energy developing and maintaining a stick-figure body. How many things do they deprive themselves of – not just in terms of food, but in life? Are they happy or exhausted from being bone-thin and empty?

Models claim it's their job not to eat, but that's not smart or healthy. When models (and people with eating disorders) diet and lose weight, often people compliment us. So we keep going and no one says anything to stop us from becoming skeletal, or from destroying our bodies and minds.

But we've become thin and beautiful, right? We should be stunningly happy, right?

Wrong.

Why? Because eating disorders do not lead to happiness.

Ever.

Eating disorders lead to isolation.

As models become pin thin, it begins to feel as though other adults knowingly participate in their demise. It doesn't feel like they're being supported. It feels like no one cares about them as a person. It feels like they've become a hanger with a paycheck.

And even if they only get out of bed for $10,000 a day, what is money going to do when their body fails? No one can go to the store and buy a brand-new, healthy body. Our bodies are our homes. If we destroy our home, where are we supposed to live?

In my teen years, I modeled. I was constantly confused as to why I was sent to auditions where girls in the hallway had boobs, when I did not. Meanwhile I was told I could lose more weight around my hips and thighs. When this was suggested, I was anorexic. I have a big Italian ass, and as my noni used to say, "Cosi facciamo?" which in her very loose translation she said meant, "What are you gonna do?"

Ultimately, what I discovered was **what strength meant to *me*.**

I used to think runway models were a symbol of strength, but I no longer admire a teetering waif that has no voice. I no longer admire or take advice from silent, stick-thin girls who I know nothing about other than one flashbulb image lying flat on a page.

Instead, to me, strength is using my voice. It's having the energy and excitement to create. It's being happy, enjoying chocolate-chip cookies, and being able to do a pull-up.

Strength is open-mouthed laughter with friends, connection, people who know my light and my dark.

Strength is running wild and free, my hair streaming behind me in the wind.

DISCUSSION QUESTIONS:

1. Have you ever had a dream you thought required you to look a certain way? How did you think being thinner would help you achieve that dream?
2. Let your intuition bring up one magazine image that had a strong effect on you in your eating disorder. When you looked at the image, how did you feel about yourself?
3. Imagine that tomorrow morning, everyone in the world wakes up with feelings of their bodies being loved, enough, worthy, and appreciated. How would this change the world? How might it change your relationship to your body?
4. What is/was your idea of strength in your eating disorder? After reading this chapter, what would you like your idea of strength to be in recovery and for your future?

ACTION STEPS:

1. Pick a magazine and go through it, image by image. List the silent messages magazines say with their pictures. Then list how many of them you see in your eating disorder. List those you can identify as manipulative lies.
2. This week, become conscious of your definition of strength. If you still live at home, look in particular at your parent or parents. Notice which behaviors, things they do, or ways of being that you see as "strong," and those you see as "weak."

11

WORTH

AN EATING DISORDER IS LIKE A CULT

Your eating disorder is like the leader of a cult. It's unpredictable. It sometimes rewards you for engaging in certain behaviors, and other times viciously punishes you for those same behaviors. It creates a constant state of anxiety where there are no moments to relax. It manipulates you to fear it, to jump when it says, and to be on guard at all times.

The reason an eating disorder holds so much power is because we have a relationship with it that's similar to a relationship with a real person.

Even smart people are taken in and brainwashed by cults. It happens slowly, over a period of time. The cult leader doesn't bang down a person's door, put a black bag over their head, drag them away, and keep them chained up until they agree to the doctrine.

Instead, cults, like eating disorders, are sneaky manipulators. They find your insecurities. They make you think they can solve them, and soon you're dependent on them for solace.

The reason you have an eating disorder in the first place is that you had an empty black hole that looked like it'd make nice home for it.

Black holes are various incarnations of the same issue: self-worth. Black holes are spaces of insecurities, imperfections, and the relentless whisper that we're not enough.

That we're worthless.

WE THINK IT CAN SAVE US FROM OUR WORTHLESSNESS

In high school, when my eating disorder started, I'd go nearly an entire school day without saying a word to anyone. I felt I didn't fit in anywhere. Anxiety exploded when I walked across campus; I prayed no one would talk to me. It was painful to make small talk because I didn't know what to say.

Most of my lunch breaks were spent in the back of the library, writing poems in my journal. I ate my lunch alone on the locker room floor and pretended to be multitasking with reading or studying if someone came by. Every lunch break, I exercised by running through the valley behind my high school. I spent hours alone, feeling alone, different, and isolated.

My black hole was feeling like I had no one. I wanted a real friend, but one who knew about my weird eating and exercise and wouldn't try to stop me. It was then that I truly began my relationship with the eating disorder.

She didn't grab me, knock food out of my hand, push me down in front of the toilet, and tell me awful things about myself. When we started our relationship, she was all compliments, smiles, and hope for a future where I was powerful and strong. She soothed me, wooed me, told me she would guide me there, and promised me the world.

Then, when I trusted her, giving her my worth and myself to her, her true colors bled through. She was cruel, but she now held my worth in her hands.

PARTS OF US ARE FOND OF THE DISORDER

Recovery is difficult because there's a part of you that doesn't want to leave your disorder behind. There's a part of you, however small, that believes it can make good on its promises, that if you just figure out how to appease her, she'll lavish you with worth and fill the emptiness.

Recovery is difficult because you had a black hole when it came to self-worth, and the eating disorder came to "help" you fill it.

But what if she leaves? What if she turns her back on you, walking out the door? Not only are you left with your original black hole, but it's been dug deeper because the one person who could "help" has written you off as worthless, too. It can feel worse than when you first began.

SEEKING INTERNAL CUES OF WORTH

Ever since I can remember, I've felt that black hole of worthlessness. In every class, I was the teacher's pet, metaphorically lying down at their feet for any scraps of praise or validation. I learned to take my cues from the external world to determine my worth. If people didn't tell me I was good, then I must not be good.

The 80s parenting philosophy was to tell kids that everything they did was good, that the picture they drew was spectacular, that they were great and wonderful. Research shows that as these children grew up, this led to a heavy sense of disillusionment when they realized they weren't good at everything.

The new philosophy is to train children to look for internal cues. For example, if Kylie draws something, instead of saying, "What a beautiful picture, Kylie. You're such a great drawer!" you would say, "I see you drew a picture. What do you like about your drawing?"

This adjustment allows the child to seek internal cues for their validation and affirmation, rather than relying on a teacher or adult to tell them they're good.

A SECRET LESSON ABOUT OUR WORTH

One of the most important lessons about worth was to me given during a guided prayer session:

> *A lot of us believe the lie that we're not good enough. Dear God, please show me the truth about this lie.*
>
> *He shows me an open field near my childhood home, one I used to walk through on the way to the public swimming pool. The field spreads out and I can see all the trees, grass, and sky. I am everywhere, spread out in molecules. He narrows in on the weeds sprouting up in tufts, with tulip buds of brownish gray feather duster puffs at their ends.*
>
> *They wave in the wind and I am filled with a secret knowing. I suddenly understand that I'm using the wrong vocabulary. I'm trying to define my worth in terms that don't exist.*

He shows me the feather duster weeds and tells me that in nature, there is no concept of "not being good enough."

In nature, the weed just is. It doesn't sit around thinking it's a horrible weed, or chastise the way it blows in the breeze.

Since we are also a form of nature, the concept of worthlessness is actually irrelevant, because we are exactly what we are made to be. You can't tell a weed it's worthless because in nature, <u>there is no word for worthlessness</u>.

We are good enough, perfect in all our imperfection, and worthy.

An eating disorder is skilled at stealing our worth. It's time to take it back.

Seek the things that make your heart sing, discover simple ways to love yourself, and fill yourself with the secret knowing that you are worthy, as is.

Developing a healthy sense of self-worth is a process that extends through recovery and beyond. We learn to nourish our sense of self with good things and love so that it can grow healthy and wise.

Where you are now is the perfect starting point.

DISCUSSION QUESTIONS:

1. How has your relationship with the eating disorder changed from when it first started?
2. Think about letting the disorder go. What are a few thoughts that race through your mind? What are the emotions or physical sensations that arise?
3. How would your life be different if you believed you were worthy?
4. What are your thoughts/feelings on the story of the feather duster weed in nature? Do we define "worth" with a vocabulary that doesn't exist in nature?

ACTION STEPS

1. Write down a few ways the eating disorder enticed you to "join" it. Include everything it promised or dangled in front of you.
2. Write out the parenting philosophy in your family. Did your parents teach you to look for external or internal cues for validation? Now write down which types of validation cues you still look for today.

12

WHAT DO YOU REALLY WANT?

THE COMMON DENOMINATOR OF ALL EATING DISORDERS

One common denominator in the development of all eating disorders is starting some sort of diet.

Diets usually begin with good intentions or healthy goals in mind. But for some of us, those same diets are the slippery slope that mark the descent into our eating disorder abyss.

The weight loss industry in the U.S. alone is a $20 billion dollar a year business[1]. Diet companies line their pockets with money they get from making you feel inadequate. Yes, I'm aware that we have an obesity epidemic in America. But for the eating disorder population, dieting is a dangerous path.

Most of us begin diets because of a focus on our inadequacies. We believe that if we weigh less, we'll be happier, stronger, sexier, better, or whatever fill-in-the-blank notion our minds have fixated on.

Take a moment to think about when your eating disorder first started. What caused you to adjust your food, or change your eating or exercise patterns?

Eating disorders don't come about in a vacuum. There are reasons an

---

[1] (http://abcnews.go.com/Health/100-million-dieters-20-billion-weight-loss-industry/story?id=16297197)

eating disorder has become our preferred defense mechanism. Often, it started because we were searching for something and the disorder promised us we could have it … if we were only a little thinner.

What were you searching for?

What did you want?

WHAT WE WANT

Wants are strange things. In coaching, I've found that people often have no idea what they want. Often when say we want something, our true want is a hundred steps removed from what we claim. For example:

- Tamera might say she wants more YouTube views or subscribers or Instagram followers … but what she really wants is to feel validated in her art and seen in her community.
- Jamal might say he wants the big promotion at work … but what he really wants is the money so he can travel somewhere relaxing with his family. He doesn't actually want the promotion; he wants a family vacation.
- Ben might say he wants the newest, trendy watch … but what he really wants is something that will give him the respect and admiration of his friends.
- Kimmie might say she wants an expensive engagement ring … but what she really wants is to feel pricelessly valued.

Often the things we *say* we want aren't what we *actually* want. There's almost always something else, something deeper.

For example, this is often what happens with eating disorders: We think we want to be skinny, that we *must* be skinny, that nothing else matters but being skinny.

But being skinny is not our true heart's desire (even if, for a time, the eating disorder convinces us it is). There's something underneath that's even more real, deep, and true.

For years I was fixated on being skinny, as if somehow that would cure all my problems. For years I had no idea there was something underneath my desire to be skinny. I simply thought I wanted to be skinny because I wanted to be skinny. Period.

UNDER THE DESIRE TO BE SKINNY

When I broke down my belief, I saw that my disorder developed during a time when I felt isolated, alone, and excluded. I invited the eating disorder in because I wanted a friend, and because she promised to make me so strong that nothing would pierce my skin.

Alas, eating disorders lie. They don't ever give you your true heart's desires. In fact, they are obsessive patterns that trap us, rather than free us.

The neat thing about God (or the universe, Spirit, whatever you like to call it) is that it can see below the things we say we want, into the things that bring us real joy.

As you progress along your recovery, I invite you to take a personal inventory of your wants.

THE PERSONAL WANT INVENTORY

The reason we first invited in the eating disorder was because we wanted something from it, even if we weren't quite sure of what it was. If we'd been aware of the thing we wanted, such as approval or love, we might have been able to get that need met in another way – one that didn't result in inviting an eating disorder in to kill us.

One of the most empowering things we can do is to be aware of what we actually want. We can do this by taking a simple inventory of our wants and desires.

Here's how to do it:

- Ask yourself, "OK, self, what do I want?"
- Answer. Say, "I want X."
- Then say, "OK, if I get X, then what do I get?" Or, "What happens if I get X? How will I feel if I get X?"

Keep going with this line of questions until you get to a root want, where you feel you've hit a stopping point. Usually this is a clearer picture of your actual want.

For example, my version:

- OK, self, what do I want?
- I want to be skinny.
- OK, and once you're really skinny, then what do you get?
- Well ... then those bitchy girls at school would stop making fun of me and I wouldn't feel so fricking helpless.
- And what would happen if they stopped making fun of you?
- I'd be ... free and powerful.
- So, what you *really* want is freedom, and to feel powerful in your life.

THEN DO SOMETHING SCARY: TELL, TRUST, & OPEN YOUR MIND

- **Tell:** Once you have your root want, put it out there in the world. Tell God, the universe, or a trusted friend about your want.
- **Trust:** Practice trust. Experience has taught me that God/something higher knows best. Trust that you'll be taken care of and that your heart's desires will show up in your life.
- **Open Your Mind:** Like Björk says, "You'll be given love" (or your heart's desires). It may not be in the way you expect to receive it. It may come from strange places, or out of the blue. But it will come to you. It's already all around you.

As you move forward on your recovery path, this process will help you see, identify, and share the things you truly want. It will also help you clarify the reasons your disorder started.

Maybe you were trying to protect yourself, so you wanted *safety*.

Maybe you were teased, so you wanted *acceptance*.

Maybe you felt invisible, so you wanted to be *seen*.

The possibilities are endless.

The gift of discovering our true wants is that we can forgive the parts of us that acted on the eating disorder. We can forgive ourselves because we see that *we were only doing our best*. We were doing what we could with what knew, to get our wants and needs met.

At a certain point in your recovery, you will know too much. Your awareness and knowledge will have built a teetering tower. This is the tipping point. From here you can only move forward because you see the lies. From here you can step back, and feel no charge when your eating disorder begins to crumble.

Awareness and knowledge are powerful. The more we dig into our recovery, the more we see that our disorder can't fill us with the things we truly want.

Trust the recovery process. Keep moving forward, even if you feel like you're going at a slug's pace. Trust, even on crappy days, that you'll get to the other side.

I have faith in you and your pink ice cream cone. You can do it!

DISCUSSION QUESTIONS:

1. When did you first have the idea that weighing less would make you better?
2. When you started the diet or change in food or exercise patterns, what were you really searching for? If a fairy godmother could have waved a wand and granted your wish, what would you have asked for at that exact point in your life?
3. Think about a time when you received something you desired, but it came about it an unexpected way. It may have taken time to realize that it had been given to you, or that you'd been given something better instead. How might this apply to the way you view recovery?
4. What are some of your true heart's desires for your recovery?

ACTION STEPS:

1. Partner up with someone you trust and take turns going through the personal want inventory with an old or recurring "eating disorder want." See if you can discover what the root want is underneath.

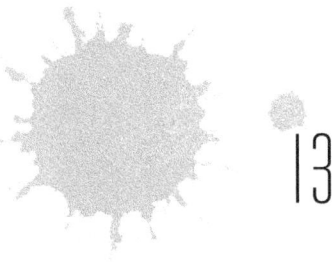

13

TRUST

IN THE THERAPIST'S OFFICE

Addictions undermine our faith in ourselves. They break us down with shame and pick away at our self-esteem. We promise we'll stop, we try and try again, but every time we fail we sink lower into the quicksand of hopelessness.

I was sitting in my therapist's office, on her black, poofy leather couch, when she said something that sounded like madness:

"You have to trust that you're going to be OK."

Alarm bells sounded through my head. Every nerve prickled. A cacophony of voices rose in the silence. My eating disorder laughed, deep shrieks exhaling like smoke from the back of her throat. My lungs constricted with a brutally honest question that rolled from my mouth:

"How do you trust yourself when you can't trust yourself?"

I'd stopped making promises years before, because I couldn't handle the heartbreak. I couldn't stomach being a worthless failure on a moment-by-moment basis. I learned not to make promises because I was a weak liar.

I had great intentions and pages of goals and dreams, but the fact was I

spent countless evenings in front of the TV shoving food down, only to bring it back up — hating myself the whole while.

HOW DO YOU TRUST YOURSELF IF YOU CAN'T TRUST YOURSELF?

When we start on our path to health, it's daunting to think about where we stand and to ponder the faraway land of recovery that other people say exists. When we're caught in the talons of our eating disorder, it seems impossible to imagine a life where we're free.

I wrote my eating disorder recovery memoir, *Throwing Up Rainbows*, because I wanted to document the time I spent in, and going through, the disorder. This was intentional. When I was in her talons, I couldn't fathom that another world existed where she wasn't present. There were few books that resonated with me, but the ones that did ended with the person not being better in the way I wanted.

I'm certain I'm not the only one who has felt this. My intention was to show a *full recovery*, not just the bright sparkly parts at the end. When I was in it, I couldn't relate to the end and it created a sad burden when people spoke of it. It was like speaking of the promised land and thinking I'd never get there.

How do you trust yourself if you can't trust yourself?

Our eating disorders have us believe that **our past equals our future**. The disorder is here and will always be here. It tells us stories of how the promised land doesn't exist, and that we're not worthy of it anyway. It tells us we're liars, we can't recover, and that we're stupid and naive to think it's possible. After all, we haven't been able to so far, right? We've tried and failed. Tried and relapsed. Tried and given up. Tried and cried.

The eating disorder tells us all about how we shouldn't and can't be trusted, so it was no wonder that the person I feared being alone with the most was myself — the one person I could never escape.

The thing is, sometimes we have to rewrite our own stories. Because the past does not, in fact, equal the future.

WE CAN TELL OURSELVES DIFFERENT STORIES

We are not failures. To say we are implies that we were, are, and always will be. We are made of particles and energy. Our cells constantly rebuild themselves. In seven years, every cell in your body will be replaced with a shiny new one. Things are in constant flux, flow, and motion.

We can change at any point in time, even if it's one cell at a time. One thought at a time. One negative story at a time.

Failure is an old, stagnant story. It's *so* one second ago (cue fashion designer inflection).

So: how do we trust ourselves if we can't trust ourselves?

WE TRUST

The answer is that we start. We begin trusting ourselves from where we are right now. It doesn't mean we have to be, or will ever be, perfect. Trust doesn't require perfection. Trust says that this is our body and mind and we no longer want to play in quicksand. Trust says we'll do the things that need to be done on our own terms.

Trust says that we'll trust ourselves to be able to handle things as they come up. We don't have to kick recovery's ass or sprint the path like a hare on speed. Trust means that we step on our path and begin to walk. That is all.

We don't have to have things figured out at all. When we come to the troll on the bridge, or meet the dragon on the hillside, or the frog prince at the lake, we get to deal with them at that time. We don't need to worry about them beforehand. No elaborate plans are needed.

When we come to each new obstacle on our path to recovery, we can deal with it then.

Until then, trust is simply walking your path. Trust is knowing that we can deal with whatever comes our way, when it arises. We'll figure it out, or ask for assistance.

We will be OK. In fact, we will be just fine.

Trust doesn't mean perfection. It means being willing to put one foot in front of the other. One foot in front of the other. Day by day. Step by step. This is how you recover.

DISCUSSION QUESTIONS:

1. How do you define trust?
2. Can you relate to the feeling of not always being able to trust yourself? How does it show up for you?
3. Are there any books that have helped you on your recovery journey thus far? What were the most important things you learned from them?
4. If you decided to start trusting yourself today, how would that trust be visible in your life?

ACTION STEPS:

1. Either journal or talk to a safe person about a time when you freaked out about something and it turned out to be OK in the end.
2. Either journal or talk to a safe person about a time you didn't know how to handle something that came up, but you figured it out and/or asked for help, and it was fine.
3. Either journal for 5 full minutes or talk for 1 timed minute about your feelings about the following statement: "You have to trust that it's going to be OK." Do you trust this? Is it something you'd like to trust?

14

SECRETS

DIFFERENT PERSON, SAME STORY

I've heard countless stories from people who've heard me speak, or who've read something I've written. Each story has the same thread: They heard/read something about my recovery, and they're secretly struggling themselves.

Often they've kept their family members, friends, or relationship partners/spouses in the dark about their secret for months or years. They're scared or ashamed to reach out. They want their struggle to end and are exhausted and sad that they're missing out on life. They want to know the secret to my recovery.

No matter how many stories I hear, my heart softens like a little marshmallow each time. It impales me to know that right now, even as you read this, millions of people are hurting. They all need help, support, guidance, understanding, and love.

I was once one of those people. I'd catch a glimpse of someone on the other side and desperately want to know how they got there.

One of the problems is that a number of women who've recovered never want to go back to that space. They live their lives moving forward, as though the eating disorder was just a blip in their past. There's no judgment in this; I understand why some people want to escape and not look back.

However, since childhood I've been self-reflective, mulling over the past, searching for meaning, needing to make sense of chaos and express it out of me. Each person who approaches me today reminds me of me, when I was caught in the disorder.

When I was still in it, I felt as though I were completely alone, trying to invent a wheel without the car blueprint.

WE ALL THINK WE'RE ALONE WITH OUR TERRIBLE SECRET

We're not, but that's what secrets do best. They isolate us and then begin to steal our joy, wiggling their way into our identity until they drown out almost everything else.

Secrets disconnect us from others because we're hiding, withholding, having to be on guard so nothing accidentally slips out.

My eating disorder was my biggest, darkest secret — the one I'd lie about to your face, and hate you for if you discovered it. The shame attached to this secret fueled my constant vigilance to keep it in the shadows. That gave it more power.

However, there's only so much self-hatred I could stand and still stay alive. As the disorder followed me into my twenties, I realized it was necessary to separate *the eating disorder* from *me*. I did this to keep a part of myself I could identify as good, because if there was *nothing* good in me, why bother?

I already had practice with creating a separate "identity," as I'd done so frequently in my adolescence. I was constantly creating different exterior personalities in order to avoid the sheer vulnerability I felt all the time. Sometimes, privately, I'd give them different names, like during my "vampire summer," when I often stayed up all night. I wanted to be an actress, so for me it was like practicing for a role. *Sage* was how I internally knew myself that vampire summer. She was mellow like honey, light, smiley, up for adventures, and lived on fruit, coffee, and conversation.

CREATING LILLIE

If I was going to have any hope of seeing myself as good, I needed to separate the eating disorder from me. So I created Lillie (notice the word *lie* is in her name). In my head, I saw her clearly. When I was anorexic, she was blond and dressed like a fairy; when she morphed into bulimia, her true self was revealed — she became dark, ugly, and vicious.

She had the energy of power, of the person who, when they walk into a room, everyone shuts up and stares at. She reminded me of a witch or sorceress, with her jet-black hair and eyes and plum purple lips that looked like she'd been kissing bruises.

Differentiating between me (the good part) and her (Lillie, the eating disorder) allowed me to hold onto a part of myself. It stopped her from laying claim to everything that was mine; she could have some things, but she couldn't have it *all*. In this way, she became both friend and enemy. But she was finally *separate* from me and had a voice I could identify — especially when I began therapy.

> *Important note: In no way was Lillie a split personality (or Dissociative Identity Disorder, formerly known as Multiple Personality Disorder), nor did I hear voices in my head. I understand (and always understood) that Lillie was an aspect of me, I simply used the form of another person to distinguish my eating disorder from the "good" person that was still me.*

Creating Lillie didn't solve my eating disorder. But it gave me something important: another entity, separate from myself, on which I could pin the eating disorder behavior. Her voice was dominant while my voice was weak. In therapy, her voice boomed. It took me a while before I could find my voice again, but that was OK.

I remember the first time a thought ran through my mind and I realized it wasn't Lillie's, because I heard it in my therapist's voice. Before my voice was strong enough to take on Lillie's, my therapist's voice was there. My therapist's voice challenged Lillie's at every turn, and slowly my voice began to wake from slumber.

SECRETS CRUMBLE WHEN WE SHARE THEM

People who reach out to me always share one thing in common: they're searching for the magic key to recovery.

The truth is, there's no one magic master key. But there are keys. Keys that unlock parts of you stronger than you could ever imagine. Keys that help you get to where you really want to be, and have what you really want to have.

One of the first keys is to share your secret with someone safe.

Secrets lose power when we share them, because we stop hiding. Secrets thrive in our darkest corners; they despise the light. Once we come out of hiding, we see that we haven't been alone in our suffering. We've just all been hiding.

Bring your secrets into the light and begin to take away their power.

DISCUSSION QUESTIONS:

1. Write a letter to your eating disorder as though it were another person/entity. What do you want to say to it?
2. What's one key you've found to help you during your recovery?
3. Who are the voices you hear in your thoughts (i.e. the eating disorder, yourself, your mother or father, spouse, or therapist)? Rate them from softest to loudest. On your recovery journey, have you noticed the volume of the different voices change?

ACTION STEPS

1. Draw or collage an image of what you perceive your eating disorder might look like. Let your intuition give it a name. What clothes does s/he wear? How does s/he carry her/himself? Do you notice anything you weren't aware of before?

2. Group: Take turns sharing some of the negative effects the eating disorder has had on your lives whether physically, emotionally, or in relationships, etc. How do you relate to other people's shares? We're not alone in this.

15

AFFIRMATIONS

THE LIGHT IN ME SEES THE LIGHT IN YOU

At a high school camp, I participated in an exercise that changed my life. Our group lined up in the middle of the forest and held each other's hands, forming a very long oblong circle, such that each of us stood facing another member of the group. In complete silence, while songs played from a boombox beside a tree, we stared into a person's eyes for a full minute. After the minute was up, the circle rotated and we faced a new person.

It's a rare thing to receive someone's undivided attention and eye contact – so rare that it can be both uncomfortable and magical.

One particular boy affected me more than the others. A deep sadness lived in his eyes. As we gazed at one another, tears formed, sliding down our cheeks. A moment later we smiled gently, with a quiet knowing. Although we were in the same grade, we'd never spoken. But in this moment of strange connection, we saw both the sorrow and the joy of one another's humanity. We acknowledged both silently, reverently.

A year later, I helped lead that same camp, organizing the counselors and creating the same magical space for a new group of people. We chose *Namaste* as our camp theme. Our t-shirt read:

> *The light in me sees the light in you.*
> *When you are in that place and I am in that place, we are one.*

SEEING OURSELVES IN THE MIRROR

I've heard that suicides are most often committed in bathrooms. I've heard it's because of the mirrors; people want to look at themselves before they die.

Looking at oneself can be excruciating or lovely. Towards the beginning of my recovery, a friend told me to stand in front of my mirror and silently tell myself, "I love you." A few days later, I took a breath, met my own eyes, and began to cry. The eyes that looked back at me were so sad, holding an innocence I hadn't protected. I thought about myself as a little kid, hair flying behind me as my Smurf tricycle barreled down a hill under a bright blue sky. I remembered being happy. I hadn't protected that.

We can't go back in time. We can, however, choose to learn. In any moment, we can learn. And a moment of learning applied is a moment of growth.

My lesson on the day I stared at my eyes in the mirror was that *I was in there*. The happy girl of Once Upon A Time was still waiting for me. So I forced myself to look in the mirror daily, to meet my own eyes, to cry if I needed to, and to smile when I felt like it.

Every day I stood in the bathroom so that I could live. So that I could find the light in myself again. So that I could connect to me.

EATING DISORDERS KEEP US SEPARATED FROM OURSELVES

It's almost as though an eating disorder draws a dotted line along our necks, forcing us to live in our heads while our bodies plod along. Although our bodies belong to us, they are unfamiliar terrain; we've been indoctrinated to believe that they're unsafe spaces. "DO NOT ENTER," says the dotted line.

Our eating disorder knows that if we enter and begin making our bodies our home, eventually we will find our way back to ourselves … and our eating disorder will be no more.

AFFIRMATIONS & CLAIMING YOUR POWER

Affirmations are now a common term. Things like, "I'm happy." "I love myself." "I love my body."

I find that often, people repeat affirmations but still feel crappy. Nothing in their life changes.

This is because when they're saying their affirmation, they don't really believe it. So, their brain is saying, "Nope," and then replacing the positive affirmation with frustration or doubt.

The power of an affirmation has to do with the *feeling generated by it*. If we absolutely don't believe the things we say, then the negative or doubtful energy we put out cancels our request.

But there's a simple solution.

Find something you *can* believe, even if you only believe it a little bit. For example, you could affirm, "I will be free," or whatever version of recovery is important to you. But you could also do, "I *could* be free."

Sometimes that one little difference of just naming the possibility feels good. You'll know what feels right because it will feel like a little grain of hope, a little warm ember burning in the darkness.

If you have difficulty finding affirmations you believe in, I recommend trying Change Me prayers. Change Me prayers are inspired by author and spiritual teacher Tosha Silver, who discovered that asking God to change her worked better than simply saying she was already there (i.e. a "regular" affirmation).

The key to Change Me prayers is this: Instead of already stating you *are* a certain way, you ask to be *changed into* someone who authentically believes the thing you want to become. For example:

- "(God/Source/My High Self), *Change Me* into someone who can overcome this eating disorder."
- "*Change Me* into someone who can love herself."
- "*Change Me* into someone who believes he is worthy."
- "*Change Me* into someone who knows her worth."

I love Change Me prayers because before I learned about them, I had my own version. It went, "Please, God, please (state my request)." For example, "Please, God, please help me get over this eating disorder." I've also used statements like:

"Please, God, please let me be free from all patterns that hold me back."
"Please, God, please help me kill Lillie." (Although this sounds violent, I thought of Lillie as a sorceress and wanted her dark magic turned back on her.)
"Please, God, please bring me happiness/peace/freedom/joy."
"Please, God, please grant me courage/wisdom/kindness/strength."
"Please, God, please bring me my wise woman."

Usually I'd end my simple prayer with, "May it be so now. Thank you. Thank you. Thank you. Amen."

WORDS ARE MAGICAL

Words have a vibrational life, which is why I always claim they're magic. The point of an affirmation is to *believe it* and for it to hold the energy of *hope* and *inspiration*.

It is said that we become what we think about most of the time. As we gather courage and walk our recovery journey, let's remember that our words and thoughts have power. Let's use our prayers and affirmations to set before us a road that is bright and full. Let's continue to walk towards the recovered life that we desire for the future versions of ourselves. When we say, "May it be so now," we can hold the vision, and the hope that one day it will be.

DISCUSSION QUESTIONS:

1. What is one affirmation you strongly believe about yourself? Why is it something that you strongly believe?
2. Is there anything you *could* believe, even if only a tiny bit?
3. What affirmation/s do you *want* to believe about yourself?

ACTION STEPS

1. Stand in the mirror and look into your eyes. What do you see there? See if you can love yourself and accept yourself as is, right now. Allow whatever comes up, to come up.
2. Write 5 positive self-affirmations on a notecard. Tape them in your house (I like the bathroom mirror) and say them out loud every morning and evening.
3. On a notecard, write the affirmations from discussion question #3 in prayer form, and ask to be a person who believes them.

16

RELATIONSHIPS

WE ARE WIRED FOR CONNECTION

From the time we're born to the day we die, we're in relationship with others. Human beings are hardwired to need connection, and we don't grow out of this as we age. Our entire lives are shaped around this hunger – we constantly seek safe emotional connection.

Harry Harlow, a psychologist at the University of Wisconsin, once conducted an experiment with baby monkeys. In this experiment, baby monkeys were taken from their mothers and allowed to choose between two "fake" mothers: a food-dispensing monkey "mother" made out of wire, or a soft cloth "mother" with no food.

The baby monkeys spent 17-18 hours a day with the soft cloth mother, and less than 1 hour a day with the food-dispensing wire one. When scared or stressed, they'd run and cling to the cloth monkey mother for contact comfort.

Even though the baby monkeys were supplied with a wire monkey mother for technical biological survival, the wire mother couldn't provide love, or emotional safety. The monkeys sought out the alternative cloth money because it felt more like a real mother, who could provide them with at least some of the emotional comfort they needed.

WE FORM A RELATIONSHIP WITH AN EATING DISORDER

The reason we have a difficult time walking away from our eating disorder is because we've woven ourselves into relationship with it. Despite the fact that it doesn't serve us, we cling to it for comfort.

An eating disorder submits us to constant mental conflict and cruel criticism, which creates a feedback loop of self-doubt, shame, and helplessness. But we stay because it's *familiar*. It's what we know.

In fact, despite its volatility the eating disorder often becomes our closest "friend." Interacting with it becomes our version of "contact comfort," like the baby monkeys with the cloth monkey. Some relate, or even refer, to the eating disorder as a "lover."

When we're in a relationship with a lover or best friend that feels chaotic, our bodies respond with elevated stress levels and depression. Yet despite this chaotic relationship, the thought of losing our connection to the eating disorder/best friend/lover sends our brain into a panic spiral.

In a previous chapter, I mentioned a few terrorizing thoughts that can surround the "fear of being fat." Even though we aren't happy, we panic when faced with the prospect of severing the relationship with the eating disorder. It's like the cloth monkey mother. It's not what we ideally want, but it has become the only comfort we've come to know. What would life be like without her? We'd enter a strange new existence.

This is OK. Panic is natural because you're contemplating losing "someone" with whom you've spent quite a bit of time and energy. You are, in many cases, losing your closest relationship. It's normal to hate her and yet grieve at the thought of being without her.

The important thing to know is that you won't be alone when you do. You can proactively set yourself up for connection, which is what you're truly seeking underneath it all. In other words, you let her go by *replacing* the destructive connection you had with her with *positive and healthy connections*.

You need connection, and you deserve connection.

You can choose to connect with others who will move forward with you into this new chapter of your life.

NO ONE TOLD ME RECOVERY WAS NOT THE END

When you've struggled with an eating disorder for a while, you wish it would just disappear. Recovery can be thought of as a finish line, and that once we get there, everything will be peaches and unicorns.

But this is the same trap we fell into with the eating disorder in the first place – that everything would be better *if*, and *once*, we were skinny.

If recovery does end up being a finish line for you, that's fantastic. Enjoy the peaches and unicorns. However, I'm pretty sure that's not how it is for most.

I spent a tremendous amount of time and energy on recovery and getting my life back. Then, as soon as I'd recovered, it seemed like most of my closest relationships (with my husband, mother, and father) imploded.

I remember saying to God, "What the f**k, God? Why didn't anyone tell me this could happen after recovery?" Then at least I could have been prepared for it, instead of feeling like someone had kicked me off my unicorn. I felt as though the "after recovery part" was kept a secret, and I also felt cheated.

The truth is, recovery is part of a larger journey towards health. Once you learn a healthy way of being with yourself, it takes time to establish healthy boundaries with others. It's a process to come back into healthy ways of relating with them, versus how you related with them before.

I would have appreciated a heads-up, so I'm giving it to you now. At the time, I took a breath and remembered my therapist's words:

"You have to trust that you're going to be OK, that you're going to be able to handle things when they come up."

RECOVERY CHANGES YOU

The thing about recovery is that *you change*. If you've truly been through it, you know yourself better than most people you'll ever meet. You've done the work, explored dark caves with flashlights, gathered and built tools along the journey. You've fought the good fight, and won.

But the fact is, no one can go through a "battle zone" and not be changed. Learning about yourself and fighting your way back to self-esteem and self-care takes courage, *cojones*, and love. You emerge from the journey having grown; you're not the same as you were before.

Often, this means that the very people who wanted us to change the most (as in, get rid of the eating disorder) are the very people who don't know what to do with the new, recovered version of us. Humans tend to resist change, even if it's positive.

Your loved ones may take time, and go through growing pains, to get used to the new you — just like it took you time and you went through growing pains to become this new you. Have compassion for others, even if they're jerks. This doesn't mean that you have to keep destructive, controlling, or negative people in your life. Use your own intuition to help you let go of those that aren't good for you. Then there will be more space to maintain connections with those that are. You can cut people out of your life if it feels bad to stay connected to them.

If you remember how difficult it was for you to change through your recovery, you can have compassion for others, while maintaining good boundaries and taking care of yourself.

A large percentage of couples don't stay together after one of the partners recovers from an eating disorder. People often separate after one person recovers, and it can be difficult. A friend of mine who recovered from anorexia, for example, emerged from recovery with a new voice and opinions, and ended her relationship because her man preferred the "before recovery" version of her. He missed the relationship in which he made most of the decisions.

It's often difficult for couples to stay together through recovery because healthy relationships require conscious energy. But it's possible. Both you and your partner can become reacquainted with the person you are now.

Recovery can also put strain on dynamics with parents, siblings, even our close friends. It can take time to figure out how to be with each other, now that the eating disorder is gone. The dance has changed, and we have to figure out how to dance to a different tune.

Also, keep in mind that recovery doesn't cancel out who you were and put someone new in your place. You are still here. It's you with a toolkit, better boundaries, communication skills, and the ability to engage in healthy self-care.

WHAT HAPPENS AFTER RECOVERY

As I mentioned, no one told me about recovery aftermath. For me, for the first time in over a decade, I felt free. I wanted to spread my wings and soar everywhere. My husband at that time, however, wanted to build a comfy little nest. We began to argue, as I accused him of being "needy and controlling" and he accused me of being "selfish."

The fighting sucked. I wasn't prepared. Flying from one side of the pendulum to the other, I refused to compromise. Part of me felt justified, since I'd felt trapped with the eating disorder for so long. I said I wanted to go to an ashram in India and travel the world with a friend. He was at a complete loss because he wanted none of these things; he just wanted to have his life, in Hawai'i, with me.

We separated for six months (not legally), and I moved out and got a place on my own. My parents took his side in agreeing I was "selfish."

My husband and I had a lot of heated conversations that teetered rapidly between "I love you," and, "I don't see how this is going to work." According to my parents, I was the bad person who was ruining everything and breaking my husband's heart.

But recovery, like recovering relationships, isn't nice, simple, or tied up with a pretty bow. It can feel like convoluted, clustered chaos. For me, there was no black or white. I wasn't the bad person, I'd just begun a different dance. A dance that had everyone thinking, "What the hell is happening!?" (including me).

The fantastic thing is that we all negotiated how to dance a new dance. It wasn't easy, but it was worth it. My husband and I ended up back together, my pendulum found the middle ground, and we got to laugh again til it filled my heart. I consider myself fortunate to have ended up with the same person who knew me through my darkness, and got to then benefit from my light. Since the writing of this recovery guide other events unfolded and we are no longer together, which is a story for another time. Still, I feel so incredibly fortunate to have had a chance to be with him for that extra handful of years after my recovery.

The truth is, during my recovery we were a fraction of a movement away from our lives going on separately. It wasn't a given for us to have had those extra years.

Not all of us will end up with our partners or in relationship with certain family members or friends after recovery, and that's OK. Some of us will, and that's fantastic. Some of us, like me, might recover and get to be with their your person for a while longer, and then separate for different reasons. Either way, at the end or beginning of a new journey you have your freedom from the eating disorder that once ruled your life.

You get to decide what's best for the new you. Think about it this way: You spent countless hours to gain your recovery, and you deserve a life that's bright and full, with people who support, love, and bring you joy.

My only advice to pass on is a gem I received during my separation (while I was in recovery). Someone asked me, "Have you done everything you can?" Ask yourself this question (if, of course, you do actually want to continue in the relationship).

Do everything you possibly can to make the relationship work. If you can honestly say that you have, with all your being, then when you walk away you'll be able to look back without regret. You'll be free from the wonder of, "What if …?" or, "If only I'd …"

If you both desire the relationship but need assistance mediating all the "stuff," couples or family therapy is a wise option. It can be transformative to have a third party who can listen, ask beneficial questions, and help direct conversations.

This couples therapy part is the step that I overlooked when our marriage got back together — and I believe it would have made a difference in the quality of the next years we had together. While we are in the throes of our eating disorder, we often forget that our partners are having their own tumultuous experience with it, as well. They, too, have their own thoughts, feelings, betrayals, and raw spots. In couples therapy, you both get the chance to address them, to hear your partner's experience, to heal old wounds, and to begin a new chapter of your marriage or relationship together. You get to start fresh with two people in your relationship (you and your partner) instead of three (two plus the eating disorder).

ENLISTING A SUPPORT TEAM

Recall the target metaphor. Often people love us and want to support us, so they keep throwing darts at the target, and we keep getting annoyed that they're not hitting the bull's-eye. However, we can't really get mad at these people for throwing love darts and missing, if we haven't told them how to hit the bull's-eye.

This is where your new skills come into play: Make a list of three or more people you'd like to enlist as your support team. Let them know you're making a support team to assist you in your recovery and beyond, and ask whether they're willing to be a part of it. Have some examples ready of what it might look like to support you.

For example, I could say, "I'd like to be able to text you at meal times, and have you get back to me at least once a day with an encouraging message like, 'You're doing great! I'm proud of you.'"

You could say, "I'd like to be able to talk to you on the phone once a week for 15-20 minutes about the healthy ways we've handled stress that week, and give feedback and support."

Whatever support you need or whatever you think might help, *ask for it*. Tell people specifically how they can hit the bull's-eye. This direct approach works especially well with family, because they usually want to help.

For example, you could say, "Mom, I don't feel comfortable taking leftovers right now. But what I would like is to stay for 10 minutes after dinner, maybe share a piece of pie or a cup of coffee with you, or just talk about our weeks."

Redirect people's love arrows so you get your needs met. Then they can do what they set out to do, which is to show they love you.

Another way to enlist a support team is to download the app Voxer. With this app, you can create groups or speak to individual people, and you can each leave voice messages that group members can play anytime. Marco Polo is another app where you can leave facetime messages in the same way but the person can see you (especially good for people who connect visually). Both are currently free.

Once you create a group of your closest supporters, when you have something you need to talk about, you can leave a message (up to 15 minutes). Then, whoever is available can respond when they're free. This allows everyone to listen and speak when they can (you don't all have to be free at exactly the same time). It also takes the pressure off any one person to respond right away, because, let's face it, we all have busy lives. It's super easy, I love both of them (as you can probably tell), and use them every day. It allows me to feel connected to — and supported by — friends I don't see often, due to our busy schedules and differing time zones.

So hippity hop to it! Gather and enlist your support team. Be clear and specific as to what they can do to support you.

DISCUSSION QUESTIONS:

1. How would you define your relationship to the eating disorder? Is it a friend, a best friend, a lover, an enemy, or something else?
2. What are your thoughts on recovery itself? What do you picture it to be like? Is it a finish line?
3. How has recovery changed you (at whatever stage you're at)?
4. What do you think your life will be like after recovery? Are there scenarios you can be aware of or prepare for in terms of your relationships with others? How might you address or prepare for them? How might you muse on them without having to have a solution at this exact moment?

ACTION STEPS:

1. Make a list of people you can enlist for your support team. Make a list of how (specifically) they can support you.
2. This week, ask at least three people on the list if they'd like to be part of your recovery team. Tell them what you'd like them to do to support you.

17

HOW TO FIND A THERAPIST YOU LOVE

BLUEPRINT TO FINDING A THERAPIST

Struggling with an eating disorder includes particularly awful days. Mine involved crying into my carpet and wishing I didn't exist.

In moments like these, when life is heavy and pressing, we're more willing to reach out for help, but often we don't know where to begin.

Eating disorders are a shameful secret, so naturally we don't want to elaborate about them to a random secretary who may answer the phone, or leave an awkward message on a therapist's voicemail.

We also know how deceitful the disorder is. By the time the therapist returns our call a day or two later, many times the eating disorder has convinced us that we don't need help, and that we were stupid to call.

Right there, a cycle is born: there's a brief, fleeting pocket of time where we're able to see clearly that we aren't healthy. But if no one calls us back in that pocket, then we're once again closed and distant to the help we desperately need.

Perhaps you've seen a therapist, but he or she didn't feel like the right match. When I first went to therapy I was both scared and elated, thinking the therapist was finally going to heal me. I soon realized I didn't like her at all, and the feeling overwhelmed me. My eating disorder laughed and said, "See? She can't help you. I'm here to stay, for good."

A licensed therapist *who specializes in eating disorders* is my tried and true recommendation for recovery. Once I had the right therapist, my transformation truly began.

Some of us will recover on our own (which is possible), but for the majority of those reading this, my guess is you've tried that many times without success. I needed a therapist for my recovery, and I'm glad I went to one. Therapy taught me boatloads about myself. Plus, my therapist was wiser than I was and able to lead me through the chaos of my thoughts and destructive patterns. I'm a huge believer in therapy. I became a therapist in part because of how much my therapist changed my life.

If you're struggling, or you've tried but haven't been able to find a therapist, know that I felt the same way. But your therapist *is* out there.

Here's how to find her/him:

1. **Technology is your friend.** Friends can give you great referrals, so ask around. However, if you're starting from nothing, begin by doing a quick Google search for "Therapists in (your area)." Psychology Today is a helpful website, as well as Psych Central's therapist finder section, EDReferral.com, and GoodTherapy.org.
2. **Check out therapist profiles.** In your Google search, a list of therapist profiles will pop up. Click into the person's profile and read their little blurb. You can learn about them and their specialty. Ideally you want someone who specializes in your issue.
3. **Go with your gut.** Make a list of therapists you think may be a good fit. List their name, specialty, and contact info.
4. **Call them at night.** Your call will go straight to voicemail. This is great, because you get to hear their voice. Think about it. This is the person you're going to be telling your most intimate secrets to. Is this a voice you want to talk to, or trust? I remember making one such call and in the first two words the person said my gut said, "Nope." So I hung up and moved on to the next name.
5. **Leave a message.** If you call and find someone you'd actually want to talk to, leave a message. Say something like, "Hi Ms. Smith, my name is Z Zoccolante and I'm looking for a therapist who

specializes in eating disorders. I was wondering if you're currently accepting clients. Will you please call me back at [your phone number — say it slowly and clearly. Pretend you're writing it down]. You can leave a message at this number, as it's my private cell phone. Once again, my number is [your phone number], and my name is Z Zoccolante. Thank you and I look forward to speaking with you." Often therapists are careful when they call you to leave a voicemail, because they're not sure who's checking the voicemail. It's nice to let them know they can leave a message with details that may identify them.

6. **Tell someone you trust that you called a therapist.** Ask him or her to follow up with you over the next week. This will keep you supported and moving forward.
7. **Make a robbery list.** Make a list of the reasons you're seeking help. What has the eating disorder robbed you of? When the eating disorder tries to convince you that you're OK on your own, you then have a concrete list to remind you that *the eating disorder lies.*

Once a therapist calls you back, thank them for returning your call. There are then two possibilities: One: they are not accepting new clients. If this is the case, ask them for a referral to a colleague and get the colleague's name and number. Two: They are accepting new clients. In this case, there are five important things to cover:

1. **Insurance**: *I have X insurance. Do you accept that fully, or is there a copay? If so, how much?* Ideally you want someone who accepts your insurance fully, unless you really like that therapist and can afford a copay or can pay out of pocket. The therapist will be able to give you more information about their specific payment and their accepted insurances.
2. **Background**: *What's your experience dealing with (your issue)?* It's helpful if their background matches yours in some way. It's easier to relate to someone who's been through a similar experience. Sometimes a therapist may not have had an eating disorder

themselves but has worked with eating disorders for years as their specialty.

3. **Type of therapy:** *What type of therapy do you offer?* The next section in this chapter outlines the most effective types of evidence-based practices for eating disorder therapy.
4. **Anything else**: Ask them any other questions or concerns you may have. Remember, this will be the person you'll be talking to about your personal experiences, thoughts, and feelings. This can be vulnerable so you want to feel comfortable with your therapist.
5. **Schedule an appointment.** Have your calendar out and ready, and do it right then. You've got momentum going and want to capitalize on it. If you really need to, you can cancel the appointment, but you want to take advantage of the window and do it now.

Good job! Once you hang up, I recommend reviewing your robbery list. This isn't just something you're putting yourself through — you're doing it for a reason. You are brave and strong. You will recover.

Finding a therapist you love is a lot like finding a good life partner. It's a person who will truly listen, ask you the right questions, call you on your bluffs, and guide you on the road to healing and recovery. There are a lot of therapists out there, and there *is* a match for you.

As you move forward, keep in mind that you can always make a different choice and change therapists. However, if you follow the steps above you have a vastly greater chance of finding a therapist you love.

LICENSED THERAPISTS — WHAT DO THE LETTERS MEAN?

When choosing a therapist, make sure they're licensed. A license means the person has gone through an extensive psychotherapy training program, has supervised experience, and has been deemed worthy by an authority to which they're held accountable.

Some common licenses are:

- LMFT or MFT (Licensed Marriage & Family Therapist). This person is also licensed to provide individual therapy.
- LCSW or CSW (Licensed Clinical Social Worker)
- LPC (Licensed Professional Counselor)
- LMHC (Licensed Mental Health Counselor)
- NCC (Nationally Certified Counselor)
- LDAC (Licensed Drug and Alcohol Counselor)

TEXT-BASED THERAPY

Personally, I encourage face-to-face therapy, and is my number one choice for anyone who asks me for a recommendation. However, not everyone prefers that (or has the option).

If time and money are a concern for you (and/or transportation to/from a therapist's office), another option is text-based therapy. This can be helpful on a number of levels, especially since it's accessible right from your living room.

Here are 3 options:

1. **RAINN (Rape, Abuse & Incest National Network)**: Free. If sexual abuse is a part of your past, you may want to consider speaking to a trained counselor at RAINN.org. They also have a telephone hotline at 800-656-HOPE (4673).
2. **TalkSpace**: ~$25/week: To enroll in TalkSpace, you ask a question on the site's homepage and enter your email. The screener therapist then pairs you with one of their 90+ registered therapists. You're able to post to your private chat space 24/7, and your therapist responds once a day. You can change therapists at any time. You're also able to set up a 30-minute live-video session for $29. Find more info at www.talkspace.com.
3. **BetterHelp**: ~$40/week: To enroll, you first fill out a questionnaire. Then BetterHelp allows you to text-chat with one of the nearly 300 licensed mental-health professionals, all of whom must fulfill the

requirements to be licensed in the state in which they reside. If you don't click with your assigned therapist, you can request a different one. You're able to share your thoughts and feelings, and your therapist responds at least once a day with thought-provoking questions. Find more info at www.betterhelp.com.

Text therapy options can be especially helpful in cases where time, money, or access to resources is limited. Most people, including teens, have personal phones and possibly laptops. Since the text chat is continuing and open-ended (instead of a once-a-week therapy session), triggers and coping mechanisms can be identified faster. Also, writing out your thoughts on your phone or laptop can be therapeutic in itself.

If you have insurance, can get insurance, or are able to find someone affordable, in-person therapy with a licensed therapist is always my first choice and my recommendation.

WIDELY-USED THERAPIES IN EATING DISORDERS TREATMENT

The therapies listed below are all *evidence-based* practices. This means they're supported by clinical evidence from systematic research. In other words, they've been tried by a large number of people and found to be successful – they're backed by data that says they work. Again, I strongly recommend seeing a licensed therapist in person whenever possible, and finding the best therapy modality for you.

1. **Cognitive Behavioral Therapy (CBT)**. CBT is the most widely-used treatment for eating disorders. It focuses on our automatic (and often negative) thoughts and beliefs, which form the root cause of the problematic thinking and behaviors that feed the eating disorder. CBT gives a framework from which to challenge and alter these thoughts and beliefs, which helps overcome destructive behaviors. CBT has proven effective with eating disorders, depression and anxiety, addiction and substance abuse, and mood

and personality disorders. It can be used in individual sessions as well as group and family therapy.

2. **Dialectical Behavioral Therapy (DBT)**. DBT is an effective therapy for people who have problems regulating their emotions, or are prone to extreme emotional outbursts. It teaches healthier ways to cope with painful emotions through both acceptance and change. DBT was originally established to treat those suffering from Borderline Personality Disorder, but has been found helpful for a number of other disorders. This is due to its education in mindfulness, stress and conflict management, identifying triggers, adjusting black-and-white thinking, and regulating self-defeating thoughts. DBT is used to treat depression, mood disorders, traumatic stress and PTSD, chemical dependency, self-injury, and sexual abuse.

3. **Acceptance and Commitment Therapy (ACT)**. ACT is based on the premise that mental distress is caused by the attempt to avoid internal experiences like thoughts, emotions, and body sensations. ACT teaches people how to observe, acknowledge, and accept these internal experiences, thus creating a better relationship with their intellect and their emotions. ACT has been found helpful for depression and anxiety, at-risk adolescents, sexual abuse survivors, and substance abuse.

4. **Exposure and Response Prevention Therapy (ERP)**. ERP helps people overcome fear and anxiety by gradually exposing a person to their feared situation, thereby gradually desensitizing their fear. It teaches those with eating disorders to be able to cope with triggering circumstances, such as eating taboo foods, *without* using the disorder behavior (binging/purging) to alleviate fear or anxiety. (This is a therapy that I'm torn about, as I believe it works but I also think there can be gentler ways to address the fear).

5. **Emotionally-Focused Therapy (EFT)**. EFT (not to be confused with Emotional Freedom Technique, from the list of somatic therapies in Chapter 18) is usually used to treat couples in

relationship distress. The goal of EFT is to create a secure attachment bond in the relationship, such that both people become a secure base for one another. Each person can then engage with world, knowing their partner is a safe haven of comfort and reassurance. EFT's success rate is between 70-75% over the long term, which is one of the highest success rates for any couples therapy. It can also be used for families and individuals, and can help treat other types of dysfunction, such as eating disorders, anxiety and depression, traumatic illness, bipolar disorder, and PTSD. (This therapy would be ideal for couples during the phase after recovery to give the relationship the best chance of success moving forward.)

FOR PARENTS AND LOVED ONES

The National Eating Disorders Association (NEDA) has a fantastic booklet specifically for the parents of someone with an eating disorder. Find it at: www.nationaleatingdisorders.org/parent-toolkit

WRAPPING UP

Today there are many different forms of therapy available. Each person is different and you will find the right form of therapy for you. I went through a few different therapists, who were all helpful, before I found the one I deeply clicked with and who I saw during most of my recovery. There are many wonderful therapist options and support systems to assist you in having a life that you love, free from the eating disorder.

Your recovery is important and you are worth it. You can do this.

DISCUSSION QUESTIONS:

1. How is therapy viewed in your family or origin?
2. If you don't yet have a therapist, what has stopped you from getting one so far?
3. Why is it important to see a licensed therapist with a specialty in eating disorders?
4. Which clinical therapy stuck out to you as something you'd like to try? Why did it resonate with you?

ACTION STEPS:

1. If you want a therapist and don't yet have one, use the information in this chapter to spend 15 minutes doing a bit of research on ones in your area

18

SOMATIC (BODY-BASED) THERAPIES

TRAUMA, THERAPY, AND THE BODY

The underbelly of almost every disorder is *trauma*. Trauma is an emotional response to a deeply distressing or disturbing experience. Trauma can occur in many forms, not just the huge ones that come to mind, like natural disasters or abuse. If an event was traumatizing to you, then you've experienced trauma.

Like muscle memory, our bodies store traumatic emotional memory. Past traumas affect our nervous system and can result in physical symptoms that disrupt our lives.

Addiction frequently has its roots in trauma. When it comes to recovering from an eating disorder, speaking to a licensed therapist with a specialty in eating disorders is a recommended priority. A popular new school of thought for addiction recovery shows that traditional talk therapy *combined* with somatic therapy gets the quickest results when it comes to recovery. This makes sense because we're not just a body, or a mind. We are multidimensional and have the opportunity to address all of us holistically, not just in part.

If you'd like to read about this connection, *The Body Keeps the Score* is a dense but excellent book that explains how trauma is stored in the body, its lasting physiological effects on the body and brain, and ways to heal. I highly recommend EMDR, Brainspotting, and Somatic Experiencing (SE) as my go-to treatment modalities to address trauma (I explain the modalities below).

PAID SOMATIC THERAPIES

Somatic therapies involve the body, or some sort of manipulation of the body. They operate on the premise that our body remembers trauma of any kind, and stores it in our tissues. Somatic therapies work by allowing our bodies to release these traumas, so our minds and bodies feel freer.

As stated, research now shows that healing from eating disorders and addiction (and staying recovered) works best when a person sees a licensed therapist *and* participates in somatic therapy. My favorite combination of therapy addresses both the mind and body using CBT and some form of somatic therapy, such as EMDR, Brainspotting, or SE. When treating both the mind and the body, complete healing is possible. Our bodies are designed to heal.

Every person is unique, and what works for one may not work for another. It's up to you to discover the way your body and mind heals best.

Here are the top 8 somatic therapies that require payment:

1. Eye Movement Desensitization and Reprocessing (EMDR)

EMDR is designed to relieve psychological stress, or as I tell my clients, "to lower the volume of upsetting and traumatic memories." Many say EMDR helped them more in one session than in years of other previous therapies. This is the way I explain it to clients, in my words: "The concept behind EMDR is that when a traumatic memory happens, let's say at age 6, the memory gets stored in a 'bubble' with all the sights, sounds, emotions, sensations, beliefs and coping skills you had at that time. Then when the 'bubble' pops, it feels as if the event is happening in real time and the body reacts as though you are six years old again. EMDR helps lower the volume on the distressing events and allow the adaptive memory network (like a river in your mind) to absorb the memory, so it becomes part of the river again instead of sitting on the top in a trauma 'bubble.'"

The neat thing about EMDR is that the client does *not* have to talk about any disturbing memory in detail. The practitioner, while in conversation with the client, uses arm movements, buzzers, or a light machine to cause the client's eyes to follow rapidly from left to right (bilateral stimulation). With the use of these eye movements, the intensity of the client's connection to the trauma is reduced.

2. Brainspotting

Brainspotting is known in the therapy community as the new modality of EMDR. It was created by David Grand, an expert practitioner of EMDR and SE (see below) who brought in the knowledge that direction of our eye position allows people to access different emotions and feelings. Brainspotting is an offshoot of EMDR, so the basis of the neurobiology is the same. The difference is that with Brainspotting, audio music is heard in both ears (bilateral stimulation) while the client is instructed to hold a fixed eye position that corresponds to the trauma being worked on. This modality can be especially good for people who have a lot of body sensations with their trauma.

3. Somatic Experiencing (SE)

SE is based on the premise that trauma is a natural part of life, and that the body is designed to heal. The founder, Peter Levine, developed SE after studying animals in the wild, and noticing they were able to avoid becoming traumatized after life-threatening interactions. Once in a safe space after a traumatic event (such as getting mauled by lion), these animals were able to self-regulate by discharging energy. They used involuntary movements such as shaking, trembling, and deep spontaneous breaths to release tension.

All these things reset the autonomic nervous system and restore balance. SE sessions are done in person and are useful for shock trauma and for developmental trauma because it doesn't retraumatize the person. A few examples of single-episode trauma are a sexual assault; witnessing or being involved in a serious accident; or losing a loved one. Developmental trauma is the result of abandonment, abuse, and neglect during a child's first three years of life. Developmental trauma disrupts cognitive, neurological and psychological development and affects attachment to adult caregivers.

4. Network Spinal Analysis (NSA, also known as "Network")

NSA uses light touch along the neck and spine to gently allow the brain and nervous system to release trauma. The goal is for the gentle prodding to assist the person's body to develop an awareness of its own tension, and self-correct.

5. Acupuncture

Acupuncture is a 3,000-year-old modality in which tiny needles are placed on the skin along specific energy channels of the body. The needles act to release stagnant energy and bring the body's energy flow back in balance.

6. Massage Therapy

Massaging the soft tissue and muscles of the body has tremendous physical and emotional benefits. It can help us become more aware and connected to our physical bodies. It's a way for our bodies to receive safe, non-sexual touch, which relaxes our body and makes it feel good. It allows us to practice doing nice things for ourselves. I'm a massage therapist, and no, we're not looking at or judging your body, we're focusing on caring for it with massage. If you're nervous about massage, ask a trusted friend for a referral, and keep in mind you can specifically request a male or female therapist depending on your preference.

7. Rolfing (aka Structural Integration)

Rolfing is a form of massage therapy that focuses specifically on manipulating the body's fascia (web-like connective tissue) in order to release stress patterns and improve the alignment and movement of the body.

8. Psychodrama

Psychodrama includes elements of theater, and offers people a creative way to explore personal problems and identify solutions. In psychodrama, a trained director oversees a psychodrama therapy group. In present time, the group reenacts real-life, past situations, or internal problems or dramas. Participants get to see their personal life events and those of other group members played out. This allows members to reflect on and understand how past behaviors currently affect them. They have the opportunity to reflect, evaluate, gain insight, and problem-solve for their own lives.

FREE SOMATIC THERAPIES

If you aren't in a position to hire a paid somatic therapist, there are a number of free therapies you can practice. However, if your trauma is particularly severe, it is strongly recommended that you engage in therapy with a practitioner, and not on your own.

Here are several somatic therapies that will help you gain a way to identify and clear emotional blocks that are stuck in your body:

1. Emotional Freedom Technique (EFT, or "tapping")

The technique of "tapping" focuses on clearing a current negative emotion by using your fingertips to lightly tap on 12 meridian points on the body.

Meridians are specific channels in the body through which energy flows. In a matter of a few minutes, "tapping" can help turn down the emotional volume of an issue, resulting in relief. "Tapping" can be used for disorders and addictions, fears and phobias, chronic pain and physical disease, PTSD, and emotional problems.

Examples of "tapping" for eating disorders:

Let's say we want to tap on "fear of getting fat." We first rate the *charge* (negative emotional intensity) of that belief on a scale of 1-10. We close our eyes, say the phrase, "I'm afraid of getting fat," and feel in our bodies how much charge it holds. If it's a 10, we are absolutely, positively terrified.

Then we do a setup statement and start tapping on each of the meridian points. As we tap, we say aloud whatever comes up when we think/feel about "I'm afraid of getting fat." Some automatic thoughts that might come up:

- I'm afraid/terrified of getting fat.
- I'll die/be disgusting if I get fat.
- Getting fat is unacceptable/unbearable.
- I hate the idea of being fat. I hate, hate, hate, hate, *hate* it.

Allow your mind to "wander." Your memories and emotions are stored in clusters, which may seem unrelated at first, but in fact are all part of the same belief *system*. It's almost as though our networks are the legs of a dog. The front right foot may be firing to run, but this front right leg movement is connected to the dogs three other legs, and they're moving as well. This means that if there's a neural network around the fear of getting fat, there are other neurons firing in sequence with that one.

What you're trying to do is get to the *root* of the terror or fear. Some possibilities are:

- I'm terrified that if I get fat, I'll be ugly and no one will love me.
- I'm scared I'll be completely powerless.
- I won't have anything special about me.
- I'm scared I won't be accepted.
- I'll be helpless. I won't be in control. I'll be hurt again.

For example, let's say you never connected your original fear of getting fat to a fear of helplessness. You may first make this connection during "tapping." When this connection is made, you might have the urge to cry, yell, curl into a ball, or whatever it is. Part of "tapping" is allowing the emotion to come up to the surface, and then expressing it. (Expression does not include self-harm or harm to another person.)

Examples of where you can tap:

- At the beach (you can also then practice underwater screams or move your body peacefully with the sunset)
- In the car (not while driving)
- On a rooftop in the middle of the city during winter (good for yelling/crying without anyone hearing)
- In the shower
- In a secluded bathroom stall, during work hours

"Tapping" can be done in a whispered voice. You can hum or sing to yourself while tears silently roll down your cheek. You can breathe the negativity out in long explosive breaths. Whatever comes up, get it out of your body. Release it. You will feel different.

"Tapping" is a powerful, free tool to help you immediately when emotion strikes. The more you practice with it, the more comfortable you become with it.

Find out more about tapping at www.thetappingsolution.com. There are videos and more instructions there.

2. Yoga

There are a number of different styles of yoga. Benefits of practicing yoga range from greater flexibility and strength, to pain reduction, to cultivating a sense of peace within life's chaos. Most importantly, yoga moves the body, and the body's energy and flow is the opposite of stagnation.

Yoga allows us to practice acceptance for the place our body is at this exact moment in time. Remember that your body is your home, and it's different every day. Eating disorders promote a disconnection from our bodies, such that we often spend all our time in our heads, and sometimes don't even know how to be in our bodies.

Yoga can create a safe space to explore and sit our bodies, which we will have for this entire lifetime.

Google "best free online yoga video" for an array of free videos you can do at home.

3. Art Therapy

Art therapy, aka expressive arts therapy, includes drawing, painting, sculpting, etc. The idea is to create something artistic that helps you express yourself.

Art therapy is often used in children's therapy. A child's language faculties aren't developed yet, so the child might not be able to speak about what's going on. However, when asked to draw it out, the therapist will often gather far more information than from the child's spoken language alone.

This is interesting because so much of the experience of having an eating disorder feels like the process of diminishing our own voice, while giving space to the voice of the eating disorder (*its* thoughts and needs). Therapy can help us find our voice that was lost or stolen by the eating disorder. Art can help us dramatically, especially because we don't have to verbalize the feelings or events. We can express them in a safe, non-verbal way.

4. Other Expression Therapies/Modalities

Journaling requires nothing but you, something to write with, and something to write on.

When we handwrite something, we not only feel the thoughts we write, but we use 10,000 different hand movements, which activates 10,000 neural pathways. When we type, we only make 8 different movements. If you can, write with blue pen on white paper (blue ink results in better retention by the brain).

Dance. Put on music you love and move your body. Your posture and mood are connected. Simply changing your posture has the ability to dramatically adjust your emotional state.

Walk. Studies show that walking, preferably in nature and for at least one hour, can reduce and relieve depression. If you can only walk for ten minutes, then do that. Look out at the world, say your affirmations, and practice gratitude.

Prayer. We are not alone in this. God (or just something greater than you) *does* want you to succeed in recovery.

You are loved. You are worthy. You are doing a great job. Ask for the belief.

We have all experienced trauma, whether large or small. An important part of healing from our eating disorder is to discover and heal those memories in our mind, and in our body. As you seek out a cognitive therapist to talk things through, also seek out a somatic therapist to release the emotions stored in the body. In both "talk therapy" and somatic therapy, each person differs as far as who they see and feel comfortable with. Find a somatic therapy that works for you in partnership with your "talk therapy." If money is a concern, include the free somatic therapies I've listed above. I truly believe that whole healing comes from addressing all parts of us - the body, mind, and spirit.

DISCUSSION QUESTIONS

1. Which somatic therapy stuck out to you? Why did it resonate with you?

ACTION STEPS

1. This week, practice "tapping" on at least one of your eating disorder beliefs.

19

THE BEAUTY OF THE CHAOS

Time passes, no matter how we choose to spend it. The clock doesn't judge our choices, but keeps a steady pace around its numbered circle, exporting time.

I'm not a numbers person. Not in math, not in life, not in my eating disorder. It was only upon reflection that I once realized it had been nearly a year since I'd thrown up. During that time, I'd moved out from the home I shared with my husband, been deemed "selfish" and misunderstood by my family, stopped seeing my therapist, and had no idea what my future held.

There were days of screaming in my car, sobbing into the steering wheel, wondering if I should snap my hands left and smash myself into the center divider. In dreams, I'd run towards a cliff's edge and hurl my body into the open air.

But I didn't throw up. I didn't throw up. I recovered.

Then, time spiraled in reverse and everything I'd lost circled back into my life — except the eating disorder.

I didn't spend time with her. I didn't think about her fondly in her absence, as though we'd reunite with kisses on each cheek. I was done with reunions, done with her plum-colored lips that left emotional bruises.

Tick tock.

As I step into the lobby, I stop at the group that has gathered to welcome a colleague back from vacation. She is dressed all in black, as though she's come from yoga class. On instinct, I smile brightly, despite my insides reeling from the sucker punch of her presence. She is skinny – tall and skinny. Her brown hair falls in curls, bouncing as she laughs, giddily brushing away the attention.

Keeping my smile bright, I make an excuse to leave. Work things. I am, after all, at work. As I walk down the hallway, I hold myself together until I close the bathroom door. Then the darkness fills my chest, pushing me down to the floor.

Something about that colleague, at that moment in time, has opened a wound. The air around me crackles like static, like someone has tuned the radio dial and voices come through muffled.

By the end of the day, I am in a full-blown frenzy. That night, at home, I can't keep still. Anxiety rises like water in a closed room as I pace the carpet, meandering from room to room, finally making my decision.

My fingers click through the search engines; I am determined to become anorexic again. My fingers are hooks and little information fish come to the surface to nibble. I scour sites and articles. I bring in paper and begin to take notes, making a rigid list of what I will eat and what I will do. I will be extra skinny again. It feels like oxygen.

By this time, my husband stands behind me, and asks me what the heck I'm doing.

"What does it look like?" I ask with a fire-sharp tongue.

A few sentences of exchange.

"Leave me alone," I say, and he sighs, his disapproval palpable.

I don't care. I'm on a mission. *I'm going to be skinny again.* I'm going to *be* something. I find more sites. People talk about what they eat, how thin they are, photograph their bodies, share lists of foods, tips, and motivation.

Then, in the middle of reading a random girl's post, it's like the frequency changes; everything from the moment before vanishes into the ether.

It's apparent in her words. Sadness begins to pull at my heart because I know: This girl is sick. This girl needs help.

These girls are sad. These girls might die.

These girls have it all wrong.

What the hell am I doing?

I sit back from the computer as though stepping out of an astronaut suit, and the world is once again normal. I laugh, a long, giggling stream escaping from me.

"What's so funny?" my husband asks gruffly from the living room. When I don't stop laughing, he gets off the couch to check on me.

"I can't do it!" I laugh. "It's a joke."

If I've ever been sure change is possible, that was the lightning-clear moment. In that instant, something snapped. I saw through everything. I realized that after all the torture I'd put myself through, after putting my relationships through a furnace, and after everything therapy taught me, *there was no way I could ever go back*. I know too much now. I see through the lies.

It was the moment I knew I was truly free.

I wouldn't have to watch my back for her return. There would be no more midnight dances, no more kissy bruises and their emotional scars, no more hiding, secrets, or shame.

Eating disorder,
I see you clearly for what you are
&
you have no power over me.

*

RECOVERY IS YOURS

It may take you a while to recover, and that's OK.

Go at your own pace. Make wide leaps, hops, skips, and jumps. Take tiny steps, or crawl, snail-like. It doesn't matter how you do it, but keep inching forward.

As a friend once told me, "The earth is round. If we keep walking, eventually our desires end up at our feet."

May your moment of knowing be the beauty of your chaos.

With Love and Aloha,
Z :)

ACKNOWLEDGEMENTS

Words are magic, and they have the power to heal and transform. To all those who have been a part of my recovery journey, who have spoken the truth with love, my heart holds oceans of gratitude. Many of the thanks in my memoir apply here as well in the backdrop. For the specifics of this recovery guide, I'll name a few:

To Mel, for editing; and for our nonjudgmental conversations on sexuality that have helped me to embrace, accept, and love the feminine and soft parts of myself. You can find her, and more information on her sex and dating research, at www.melaniecurtin.com.

To Lisa Chaly, @Lisachalyphotography, for her many talents, including the original cover photo and many fantastic photo shoots.

To Marisa Bean, @thecornerphotography, for creative logo design.

To Adam Siddiq, for the ease you bring in guiding the vision.

To Liza Wacker, the therapist who taught me how to sit with uncomfortable feelings, explore the shadows, make friends with them, and discover their wisdom.

To Leon, who once upon a time was my number-one fan. Thank you for your steadfast belief in me and for confronting my disorder in the light, which forced me to make choices to stay and recover. With you, I felt so incredibly loved. My heart holds silent wishes but mostly it whispers, *thank you*.

To my family, who I'd hands down choose again if I had to do it over.

To God, and Jesus, who walked with me through shadows of death and holds me in the palm of his hand.

To Lillie, my eating disorder, thank you for trying to protect me back then. I'll always be grateful for the person I became because of what I learned.

To Di, in all of the universe I feel extraordinarily blessed for our friendship.

To all those who've come after, for showing me more of the beautiful things and teaching me how to play large and live in happiness and freedom.

For those on the recovery journey, you're the reason this book exists. Keep going — freedom is at your fingertips.

Z Zoccolante loves belly laughs, starry skies, honey lattes, and is deeply fascinated by a well-written fairytale villain. Originally from Hawai'i, she lives in LA working as a therapist, specializing in freedom from addiction and trauma, writing screenplays and novels, and pursuing other creative adventures. Find her recovery podcast Throwing Up Rainbows, on iTunes and her recovery memoir, *Throwing Up Rainbows: My Disorder and Other Colorful Things,* on Amazon.

Visit her at ThrowingUpRainbows.com and ZZoccolante.com.

www.ingramcontent.com/pod-product-compliance
Lightning Source LLC
Chambersburg PA
CBHW020300030426
42336CB00010B/840